Tank Commander

Tank Commander

From the Fall of France to the Defeat of Germany

The Memoirs of Bill Close

Foreword by
Christopher Dunphie

Pen & Sword
MILITARY

First published in Great Britain in 2002 by Dell & Bredon as *A View from the Turret*

First published in this format in 2013 by
Pen & Sword Military
an imprint of
Pen & Sword Books Ltd
47 Church Street
Barnsley
South Yorkshire
S70 2AS

ISBN 978 1 78159 187 1

A CIP catalogue record for this book is available from the British Library

Typeset in Ehrhardt by Phoenix Typesetting, Auldgirth, Dumfriesshire

Printed and bound by MPG Printgroup, UK

Pen & Sword Books Ltd incorporates the Imprints of Pen & Sword Aviation, Pen &
Sword Family History, Pen & Sword Maritime, Pen & Sword Military, Pen & Sword
Discovery, Wharncliffe Local History, Wharncliffe True Crime, Wharncliffe
Transport, Pen & Sword Select, Pen & Sword Military Classics, Leo Cooper, The
Praetorian Press, Remember When, Seaforth Publishing and Frontline Publishing

For a complete list of Pen & Sword titles please contact
PEN & SWORD BOOKS LIMITED
47 Church Street, Barnsley, South Yorkshire, S70 2AS, England
E-mail: enquiries@pen-and-sword.co.uk
Website: www.pen-and-sword.co.uk

Contents

Acknowledgements

Among the many people who have helped me in writing this story, I would particularly like to thank my wife, Pamela, for her encouragement and general forbearance during these past few months.

I am indebted to my daughter Joanna for all her hard work in translating my appalling handwriting, for correcting my bad spelling and for compiling the manuscript in a readable form. Without her assistance the book would never have been completed.

I owe a debt of gratitude to John Westover for providing facsimile facilities.

I am thankful to two old comrades-in-arms, Johnny Langdon and John Pearson, for their help in providing background information for some of the action mentioned in the book. Their memories are far better than mine.

Not least, I would like to thank all those tank crew members who served with me throughout the war, without whose bravery, help and loyalty I would certainly not be here to tell the tale.

The publishers would like to thank Brigadier Christopher Dunphie for his help in producing this new edition of Bill Close's book.

Foreword

Throughout the 1950s, 1960s and 1970s, students at the Staff College, Camberley, were taken, as a break in the middle of an intensive year, to visit the Normandy battlefields. Here they heard, and were invariably captivated by, the stories of some of the 1944 battles, told, with dignity, humility and humour, by those who took part in them. One day was given to Operation Goodwood, the huge tank battle, east of Caen, that took place on 18–19 July 1944. The team of speakers was led by Major General Pip Roberts, commander 11th Armoured Division and generally accepted as the finest armoured commander in the British Army during the Second World War. Among the stars – and they were stars, as speakers as well as soldiers – was the commander of the leading squadron of the leading regiment of the leading brigade in that vast tank armada – Major Bill Close, OC A Squadron, 3rd Royal Tank Regiment.

Reading histories of modern warfare, where battlefields cover large areas, one is often led to believe that General X won the battle of Y. This is usually misleading: General X may have made an excellent plan, and he may have generated great confidence in his men, but at the end of the day the battle was won by the men who had to put General X's plan into effect – the men at the front. It is the fighting soldier who wins battles, and he does so, in no small degree, in response to the personal leadership provided by his squadron/company commander. This is the most personal of all levels of command. And soldiers are very quick to judge a leader. If he gains their respect, they will follow him anywhere; if they consider him to be hesitant and uncertain, so will be their performance in battle.

Bill Close was, without doubt, an inspiring and hugely respected squadron leader. To have escaped from the disasters of Calais, Greece and Crete, before he took command of A Squadron, is remarkable enough, but to have survived most of the Desert Campaign and all of the North-

West Europe Campaign, always as a front-line leader, seldom out of contact with the enemy, is astounding. Countless times his tank was knocked out, but he never saw this as an opportunity 'for a breather in the pavilion'. He simply took over another tank and continued to lead. I doubt whether the modern 'stress counsellor' would have held his attention for long! *Tank Commander* is a marvellous account of leadership at the front. How lucky 3RTR and A Squadron were to have him. How lucky were those of us who heard his Goodwood story. How lucky we all are that this outstanding soldier put his experiences on paper.

Christopher Dunphie

Abbreviations

AP	armour piercing
ATS	Auxiliary Territorial Service
AVRE	Armoured Vehicle Royal Engineers
BEF	British Expeditionary Force
DCM	Distinguished Conduct Medal
DSO	Distinguished Service Order
GHQ	General Headquarters
HE	high explosive
KDG	1st King's Dragoon Guards
KSLI	King's Shropshire Light Infantry
OCTU	Officer Cadet Training Unit
OP	Observation Post
RAC	Royal Armoured Corps
RASC	Royal Army Service Corps
RB	Rifle Brigade
REME	Royal Electrical Mechanical Engineers
RHA	Royal Horse Artillery
RHQ	Regimental Headquarters
RQMS	regimental quartermaster sergeant
RT	radio-telephone
RTR	royal tank regiment
RSM	regimental sergeant major
SP	self-propelled

Introduction

Paderborn: A Time for Reflection

The bands played 'My Boy Willie', the Queen took her place on the saluting dais, and all eyes switched to the massive new Challenger tanks roaring across the well-cut turf of the old panzer training ground.

The place: Paderborn; the year: 1985; the occasion: the presentation of guidons (similar to infantry colours) to the Royal Tank Regiment.

It is always the same with a parade of armour. The machines, not the men, seize the imagination. Onlookers get a vague vision of the figures standing to attention in the turrets, generally wrapped in blue fumes from the vehicle in front, although it is the big gun and the whirling tracks that dominate, the display of power that stamps itself on the memory.

I got into a Challenger that day, and expressed disbelief at the relative positions of gunner and breech, though I was assured that there was no recoil to worry about. The rest of the equipment I saw was just as remarkable.

In terms of fighting effectiveness, the Challenger and the first tank that I drove were as different as a bow and arrow and a machine gun. As for the men – they were young and immaculately turned out: black overalls pressed, coloured cravats indicating their unit – green for the 3rd Tanks, blue for the 4th and so on. It was clear that they knew their job too. They answered questions with the confidence of TV chat-show presenters. Bovington, the home of the Royal Armoured Corps (RAC), had done well by them. They were all highly trained in handling their sixty-ton mobile weapons platforms.

Unlike the tanks, however, there was little change in the appearance of the troopers. They hadn't grown extra heads so that they could think faster (computers can do that for them) or extra hands to push the

1

imposing array of switches. They retained the same old shape as the rest of us – two legs, two arms and the usual attachments.

In the 3RTR's sergeants' mess, where we had been invited for a drink, one of the other relics of bygone days asked me: 'Well, Bill, what do you make of them?'

Before I could think of an answer, he provided one of his own: 'They look a nice lot . . .' he said.

A little unspoken debate took place. We were both wondering how this 'nice lot' would measure up to some of the other sergeants' messes we had known. How would they have fitted into our primitive cruisers and coped with their inherent weaknesses? How would they have behaved when the hull glowed a dull red under the impact of solid shot that had travelled just too far to penetrate?

There was no doubt about the answer to the first two queries: they would have coped. But the last one – that's something you only learn for certain on the day. You can check out a machine with other machines, test it to destruction if you like, but you can't do that with your own soldiers. The enemy does that for you.

Somewhere near the Dortmund–Ems Canal, three weeks before the end of the war, a determined but misguided German soldier stood up in his slit trench, shouldered his panzerfaust and let fly into the side of my Comet. There was an almighty bang, my heart leapt, and I scrambled shaken and angry down the hull through thick clouds of stinking smoke.

The pent-up tension in the turrets of the squadron immediately erupted into a storm of Browning fire. The German tried to surrender after doing his bit for the Führer, but he had sadly misjudged the situation.

There had been a time in the desert when a certain spirit of 'live and let live' applied, when it was considered 'bad form' to machine-gun a crew that managed to get out of a panzer or M-13. Once a tank had been disposed of, honour was satisfied. If anyone was lucky enough to escape from a 'flamer' or battered hulk, good luck to him.

The 21st and 15th panzer divisions, and the Italian Ariete armoured division, had subscribed to this code of chivalry for a while but by the time we arrived on the banks of the Dortmund–Ems Canal, the semi-sporting attitude which had characterised the desert campaigns had vanished. That unknown hero with the bazooka was dealing with a lot of worried, anxious men. There were no eager candidates for the position of lead tank, lead troop or lead squadron in 3RTR by April 1945. Whether a man had been at the sharp end for five years or only five weeks, all he wanted to do was to get safely through what were clearly the closing days of a drawn-out and bloody conflict. It would be a victory for the soldier only if he survived. Then he could go home and show his scars, wear his medals, and grow old. Otherwise it had been a waste of effort, uncomfortable and unrewarding for most of the time.

In the closing stages of the campaign in North-West Europe, great care had to be taken to keep rotating units so that everyone took it in turns to head the advance. Though the opposition was dwindling, it was erratic, and we knew that it would be the point tank or troop that would suffer if we bumped into a detachment of unrepentant Nazis. Hence my orders that no chances were to be taken where bazooka men were concerned. If any did survive the hail of bullets, they would undoubtedly pass the message on to their friends.

My crew emerged from the wreck unhurt that day on the Ems Canal. It wasn't always like that. For me it was the eleventh time I had been 'shot out' of a tank.

This account is a personal account, based on my own experiences as a tank commander, as a member of 3RTR throughout the war. The main incidents of the story are based on facts; if at times the details are at variance with military histories, that is merely because, with the years, memory becomes a little dim.

In order to give my story 'life' and perspective, it is necessary to digress a little and give you a brief summary of my history and movements up to the time of these adventures.

In 1939 I was a sergeant in 3RTR, a regular soldier of some six years' standing. On that fateful morning of 3 September, as we learned that we were at war with Germany, it would have been impossible to hazard a guess at what fate held in store for us. I could not have had the slightest inkling of the thousands of miles I would travel with the 3rd Tanks or the many escapades that would befall us during the next five years. It was to be five years of continuous travel, of continuous fighting, for, no matter where the 3rd Tanks went, they were usually in the van of the attacks, often rearguard in retreat, but always in the thick of the fighting.

My baptism of fire was at Calais in 1940 where, unfortunately, after withstanding six days of continuous siege, most of 3RTR was 'put in the bag'. Some 250 officers and men were able to slip away and get back to England. I was one of the lucky ones.

In November 1940, refitted and back up to strength, we were sent to North Africa and figured in all the battles: the bloody fighting at Sidi Rezegh, Bir Hacheim, Knightsbridge and the battle of the Cauldron. We led, in part, the advance to Agedabia and Msus, and went back again to Alamein. We took part in the famous 'left hook' battle and the forcing of the Gabes Gap and the Mareth Line, the entry into Tripoli, and the relief of Tobruk; all these names mean much to the men of the 3rd Tanks.

Throughout these battles, essentially tank battles, the 3rd Tanks played their part. In 1941, just after we had started out on Wavell's first desert advance, the battalion was withdrawn from the line and sent to Greece. There, after some four months of active service up in the north, where our tanks were neither strong enough nor numerous enough to stop the onslaught of the Germans, the remnants finally collected themselves in the glades of Glyfada and Daphne near Athens, prior to evacuation. Some 200 officers and men of the battalion eventually landed back in Egypt after various exploits.

I, with some sixty men of the unit, was left behind in Greece, given up for lost. However, after a perilous trip across the Corinth isthmus, lying up in the hills during the day and coming down to the beaches of southern Greece at night in the hope of being picked up, we eventually managed to get away. We were taken offshore by the destroyer *Hotspur*, but on our way we were badly hit by Stuka bombs and all the evacuees put ashore on Crete. The *Hotspur* was finally sunk by further bombing, not long after we had left her.

After various adventures in Crete, we were extremely lucky in making our way from Crete to Alexandria on an old Greek steamer that had been lying idle for some months. The ship, named *Popeii Veronica*, eventually brought us back to Egypt after a trip lasting five and a half days. Our fuel ran out a little way off the coast of Egypt and we literally had to tear up the decks and outhouses to use as fuel to get ourselves into port.

We then joined the remnants of the battalion who were in camp on the outskirts of Cairo and were in the process of being refitted. In Greece we had lost some 450 officers and men – killed, wounded and POW. However, there were still enough of us to form the nucleus of almost a new battalion. By this time I had been promoted squadron sergeant major. We spent the next few months training our new crews and taking over the new American tanks, the Honeys.

In March 1942, just prior to going 'up the blue' – moving from base camp to the battle zone – in readiness for expected operations, I was granted an immediate commission. Rather unusually, I remained with the same battalion and merely walked out of the sergeants' mess and into the officers' mess. After the battles and marches through to Agedabia for the second time and the eventual retreat back to Alamein, I had reached the rank of captain. At Alamein I was second-in-command of a squadron and then later, during the famous 'left hook' battle of Gabes, when my squadron commander was wounded, I took over command of A Squadron from then until the end of the campaign in North Africa. In March 1943, exactly one year after commissioning, I was promoted to major. I was one of the very few officers or men still serving with the battalion who had been with the unit since the outbreak of war.

In November 1943, after enjoying a spell of five months' leisure at Horns on the North African coast, we left for the UK. We had a most enjoyable trip through the Mediterranean and arrived home in time for Christmas – our first Christmas at home for three years.

After a period of training with new tanks – Shermans this time – on the Yorkshire moors, we were ready, or so we thought, for more action. We were part of the 29th Armoured Brigade in the 11th Armoured Division. Our brother units were the 23rd Hussars and the 2nd Fife and Forfar Yeomanry. Neither regiment had, as yet, been bloodied but they were extremely keen and well trained. By June 1944 we found ourselves, in company with thousands of others, in a transit camp in the south of England, awaiting orders for the big day, the long-awaited D-Day.

On 12 June 1944 we landed back in France on the beaches of Normandy, this time in a very different frame of mind: fully determined to avenge our ignominious retreat and evacuation of 1940. Of our battles during these first few weeks in Normandy I will say little. The type of country in which we found ourselves was very different to the open wastes of the desert. The fighting technique we had learned through bitter experience in North Africa was of no use here. We had to re-adapt ourselves to an entirely different type of warfare. In particular, we found the narrow lanes and high hedges of the bocage country presented new problems for tanks.

In the following pages I have tried to describe in more detail the actions of men in battle, the frustrations, the elation of success, but, most of all, the comradeship which existed among the men who fought in tanks.

A number of senior officers with experience of the big Second World War tank battles are still alive and can describe events up to brigade and divisional level. My perspective is restricted to the view from a tank turret. The most unusual thing about it is that it spans five years in the same unit – the 3rd Battalion of the Royal Tank Regiment – which I had joined as a regular soldier before the war. In 1939 I was a troop sergeant, in 1941 I became a squadron sergeant major, and then I was commissioned in 1942. Normally a soldier, NCO or warrant officer went away to do an officer cadet course and, on posting, joined a different unit. This avoided possible embarrassment with former comrades – or superiors. I just carried on.

To modern 'tankies', I remain something of a curiosity because when 3RTR spearheaded the massive armoured assault launched outside Caen in July 1944, I commanded one of the lead squadrons. All young officers study this controversial battle and, until recently, the Ministry of Defence ran excursions to the scene, with old soldiers from both sides present to relate their experiences. Now these 'battlefield tours' have been dropped for economic reasons and a film has taken their place. The 'old and bold', such as myself, are sometimes invited to the Staff College at Camberley to add our comments.

Though we went through hard times, such as during Operation

Goodwood, 3RTR did well in Europe. There were none of the unqualified disasters that I witnessed in earlier days. Paradoxically, the more we looked certain to win and the better our tanks became, the more the crews needed maintenance. An entry in my pocket diary sums up the situation: 'Corporal Jones is looking a bit bomb happy . . .' At the beginning of April 1945, 1,000 British tanks were advancing from the Rhine bridgeheads. By 6 April, some 125 had been wrecked beyond repair and 500 others had suffered enough damage to keep them off the road for more than twenty-four hours. And this was when the Wehrmacht was crumbling, even desperate.

Major causes of 'bomb happiness' are the enemy, the weather and the Staff. The first sets out deliberately to make your life a misery; the second is a natural and neutral phenomenon in league with the opposition; and the third is absolutely unpredictable and sometimes seems to possess all the adverse tendencies of the others.

I commend this thought to the keen young men from whom the army expects to recruit the commanders of the future. They know that if anyone is fool enough to start another European war, it will probably begin conventionally where the last one left off – with a massive armoured battle on the North German plain. I say 'probably' because I am inclined to believe a shrewd old German general, who said something to the effect that, given three options, the enemy will usually choose the fourth.

Green Tabs

This song was composed by Major J D Dunlop, MC. It was sung during the Second World War to the tune of an old sea shanty, 'Wrap me up in my tarpaulin jacket'.

I joined up when they called us The Tank Corps,
And drilled upon Bovington square,
And The Third Royal Tanks I must thank for,
The blessing of Lydd's salty air.

Oh, I wear a Green Tab on my shoulder,
And a little White Tank on my arm,
'Twas The 3rd Tanks that taught me to soldier,
And with them I'll come to no harm.

They gave me an A10, and I drove her
From Fordingbridge to the train,
And we matelo'd to Calais from Dover,
And soon matelo'd back again.

Oh, I wear a Green Tab …

Then shortly we formed up to be shipped
On a voyage that lasted for weeks,
And we'd just learned the language of Egypt,
When we sailed off to fight for the Greeks.

Oh, I wear a Green Tab …

Still we came back and fought in November,
At a place they call Sidi Rezegh,
It's a name I shall always remember,
It's memory still keeps me awake.

Oh, I wear a Green Tab …

When Rommel retired, our gun barrels
Were trained upon Agedabia,
And at Christmas the sweetly sung carols
On the wireless, brought many a tear.

Oh, I wear a Green Tab …

At last we pulled out of the swelter,
And forgot all the woes of the 'Blue',
And dawdled about in the Delta,
Doing all that we'd wanted to do.

Oh, I wear a Green Tab …

But soon some more tanks did appear,
And we rolled on the flat cars again,
And we set out for Bir bu Menfia,
And sang to the jolts of the train.

Oh, I wear a Green Tab …

One morning in May at Igela,
We met our friend Rommel again,
As a rest cure the show was a failure,
So we walked back and sang this refrain.

Oh, I wear a Green Tab …

9

Well, Rommel got ruder and ruder,
And so did the Ninetieth Light,
But the Gunners got warm at El Duda,
So we all got away in the night.

  Oh, I wear a Green Tab …

Now at Knightsbridge I suffered a 'Trauma',
At Harmet I learned how to brew,
And I walked home again at Acroma,
And sang with the rest of the crew.

  Oh, I wear a Green Tab …

As we motored the minefields by moonlight,
In the area south of Tobruk,
Although I knew friend Rommel soon might
Attack, I did not bother to look.

  Oh, I wear a Green Tab …

Then at Sidi Rezegh in the sunlight,
They all looked like 'Honeys' to me,
Yet it turned out an 88 gunfight,
And the 'Honeys' were Mk IV and III

  Oh, I wear a Green Tab …

At length we drew back to Imayid,
And the rest we were glad to receive,
As we sat there we dreamed and we sighed,
For Alex and Cairo and leave.

  Oh, I wear a Green Tab …

At Quassassin Camp with the Cavalry
Division, in 8th Armoured Brigade,
We indulged in some riot and revelry
Then we went to stop Rommel's last raid.

    Oh, I wear a Green Tab …

Now that was the first fight for Monty,
Since then we have fought many more,
And we're sure if he does what he
Wants to, Eighth Army will soon win the war.

    Oh, I wear a Green Tab …

Chapter One

1933: A Call to Arms

'Somehow Will, I don't think you're cut out to be either a chemist or a dentist,' said Mr Bayley who performed both functions in the little market town of Uppingham where we lived. He was looking at the wreckage of the chair. He didn't seem to mind about the glazed ceiling I had fallen through (his dental room ceiling); it was the chair that bothered him. It was brand new, his pride and joy – adjustable head rest, touch here for up, press there for down, swivel with ease.

'You wouldn't think it would break so easily.'

'I don't suppose you would, Will.'

He was a nice man. He paid me fourteen shillings a week and gave me a day off to study maths – private tuition for which he also paid. Mr Bayley had been understanding about the new delivery bicycle too but that was more easily mended. When I told him some time after the chair incident that I had signed on for the army, he said that it was probably a good thing.

'No vacancies in the 11th Hussars, my lad,' the sergeant said at the recruiting office in Stamford.

'What about the 9th Lancers?'

'Fully subscribed . . .' He thought for a minute. 'Tell you what. Why not join the Royal Tank Corps? They need bright lads.'

I hadn't much idea about the Tank Corps but I agreed all the same. The recruiters gave me a short test in English and maths and I signed on the dotted line, received the 'king's shilling', and left with instructions to report to Bovington Camp in Dorset. When I told my parents what I had done, only my mother seemed to have doubts. My father, who was struggling to make a living out of a pub in which he had a part share, agreed with Mr Bayley – probably a good idea. The Depression was at its height and steady jobs were hard to find.

I don't think a single one of the thirty-four other recruits in Squad 386 had ever heard of Uppingham, or even of Rutland. Most of them were English, but there were five Scots, four Welshmen and three Irishmen. Jock Pennycuick, who had his bed next to mine in the barrack-room, could have been a Chinaman for all I knew. He was a Glaswegian and I never understood a single word he said during the whole of our training.

Paddy Davis on the other side bothered me because he confided that he had joined up only so he could learn about weapons in the shortest possible time. He was a member of Sinn Fein (whatever that was) and was going to join the IRA. I only half believed him, but he deserted after twelve weeks and much later I heard he and his brothers had been killed while carrying out some terrorist activity.

Barrack life was pretty awful in those days: no privacy and rotten food. The squad occupied two connected huts and its members spent much of their time fighting amongst each other; I was glad I was fairly athletic and useful with my fists.

After three months' initial training we were given a weekend pass to go home, having turned out with khaki spotless, buttons gleaming, belt snow-white, puttees immaculate and boots which had been 'boned' with a toothbrush handle for hours so they shone like mirrors. Each vision of martial splendour was capped with a black beret bearing the corps badge – a First World War tank within a laurel leaf – and the motto 'Fear Naught'. Sergeant Lemon, known as the 'Blond Bastard of Bovington' and his henchman, Corporal Fitzpatrick, had at least made us look like soldiers. As for fearing naught – we certainly had a healthy respect for our teachers. It had been a question of drill and more drill, polish and scrub, scrub and polish, with table-tops whiter than white.

After our brief leave we began drilling again, spending every morning marching about as a squad, but to flag signals instead of shouted orders. That was how tanks still communicated; if there was wireless, we certainly didn't see it.

In the afternoons we learned to drive the Vickers Marks I and II over the sandy Dorset heathland. These handy little tanks had been produced in the early 1920s and weighed between twelve and fourteen tons (there were variations). With a crew of five, they could do eighteen miles per hour and carried a three-pounder gun and up to six machine guns.

For some weeks we poured shot and shell and belts of .303 into the hillside at Lulworth Camp, on the coast down the road from Bovington. On fine summer days I used to speculate on the possibility of adventures on the North-West Frontier where there were armoured car squadrons. The thought of any other sort of war didn't really occur to me. Other romantic notions were inspired by a slight figure on a powerful motorcycle who hurtled round the narrow lanes: T E Lawrence – Lawrence of Arabia – remained a subject of mystery and fascination. We were baffled to know why anyone who had reached the dizzy heights of lieutenant colonel and become a national hero, should ever have wanted to join the Tank Corps as a trooper, or the RAF as an airman. Why should he want to tuck himself away in the cottage behind the mass of rhododendrons on Cloud's Hill that we passed regularly? He seemed to live a lonely and secret existence and I don't remember anyone – certainly none of my acquaintances – ever exchanging a word with him. News that he'd been killed came as a real shock – on the road leading to the camp, he'd swerved to avoid some children and crashed, they said. Those of us chosen to form part of the guard of honour at his funeral in 1935 spent some time learning to go through the motions of 'Rest on Your Arms Reversed!' with .45 Colt revolvers.

My posting to 3rd Battalion, Royal Tank Corps in early 1934, stationed at Lydd in Kent, was most welcome and a relief following the rigorous training at Bovington Camp. It was also the start of a relationship with the unit that would take me through the whole of the Second World War.

The incidents I shall relate are some of the many that could be told of the '3rd Tanks' and of the men who fought and died in tanks in the Second World War. It is the story of the men who fought at Calais, on the beaches of Normandy, and in the desert battles of 1941 to 1943, in Greece and Italy.

Chapter Two

Fordingbridge: A Time for Counting

The balloon went up while we were sitting in the lounge of the George at Fordingbridge watching the coots skidding over the surface of the Hampshire Avon. It was a cool grey evening. A regimental policeman stuck his head through the door and said: 'All 3RTR personnel report back to camp immediately.'

There were half a dozen of us, sergeants and wives, and we weren't altogether surprised. A few days earlier our tanks had been loaded onto flat-cars and transported with all our heavy equipment to be put aboard a steamer. The battalion was due to join the 1st Armoured Division assembling 'somewhere in France', in fact just south of the Somme. For more than a week the BBC had been reporting a situation of growing confusion and fierce fighting across the Channel and we expected to be sent for.

What was startling was the news that we would be moving out at 10 p.m. It was then 8 p.m. on 21 May. There had been no warning notice and the men of the battalion were scattered throughout the surrounding area. Messages had to be flashed on the cinema screens at Ringwood and Salisbury; cafes and pubs were scoured. The colonel came racing back from Bournemouth where he had taken his wife for dinner. It was midnight before the crowded train pulled out of the little country station and a number of men were still missing. Many wives, including my own – Josie and I had been married for six months – were living in billets in Fordingbridge and came to see us off. There were a few tears but most of the girls put on a brave face.

We were puzzled when the blacked-out train steamed on and on through the countryside: we had expected a fairly swift trip to Southampton. The next morning we were rumbling through hop fields

15

and shortly pulled into Dover. There was no sign of the *City of Christchurch*, the ship carrying our tanks.

An irreverent voice shouted: 'Look at Reggie – he doesn't look at all happy!'

'Reggie' was the CO – Lieutenant Colonel R C Keller, who had taken command in October 1939. A staff car was waiting at the station and whisked him away. The colonel looked even gloomier when he returned clutching a bundle of envelopes. None the wiser, we filed aboard the *Maid of Orleans*, a Southern Railways cross-channel steamer. We were happy not to have to carry our kit-bags, which had been stored separately.

Until the moment we cast off, at 11 a.m., anxious figures were hurrying across the quayside to the ship, having made their own way to the port. They clambered aboard to ribald shouts from their pals, who seemed to be of one mind as to what caused them to miss the train. Up to then, it was still good fun. We crowded into the saloons, packed the corridors and decks, and speculated wildly as to where we were going. A company of sappers and some London territorials, who belonged to a battalion sailing in another ship, knew nothing either.

'We're supposed to be motorcyclists,' a sergeant in the Queen Victoria's Rifles told us, 'but we've had to leave our machines behind.' Like us, they were armed with nothing more potent than their revolvers.

We told them we had no idea where our tanks were and everybody had a good laugh. The general consensus of opinion was that the army was overdoing it as usual and when we got to wherever we were going, we would sit around for days, wondering what all the rush had been about. Our minds were still conditioned by stories of the Great War. Sometimes the Germans had been winning, sometimes the British and French, but it had all worked out in the end, even though there had been some nasty moments in 1918. Now the Phoney War was over, things were only just starting.

Whistles sounded.

'Right, gather round.'

We assembled by squadrons, more or less, and were told our destination. It would be Calais.

'Our tanks will be delivered there and you will prepare them for action immediately. Light enemy armoured forces have broken through somewhere to the north and we will find them and deal with them.'

So there would be no training period 'behind the lines'. There was no more talk about joining the 1st Armoured Division.

'I thought this was supposed to be a pleasure steamer,' cracked 'Socker' Heath, a troop sergeant. He had once knocked out four men in a night in the army boxing championships.

As we steamed slowly through the dense mist we argued over what we would do if the ship carrying our tanks was sunk before she reached Calais. There would be nothing for us to fight with. 'Tubby' Ballard pointed out that if the *Maid* went down, there would be no one to drive the tanks even if they did arrive.

I had a rapport with Tubby, who came from somewhere in Northamptonshire and was one of the few people who had ever heard of my own county of Rutland. Earlier that year we'd been billeted together with a nice family at Hitchin.

The little convoy crawled on. Muffled thumps shook the blanket of fog. As it lifted, the outlines of the escorting destroyers sharpened and we made out the coast. People waved to us from promenades. Someone who had once been there on a day trip identified the clock tower of the town hall at Calais. Dark smoke was rising over the docks. By the time we tied up only a few bombs had fallen around the harbour station, but nearly every window had been blown out. British and French soldiers and dockers were crunching about aimlessly on a sea of glass.

'Stay where you are,' we were told.

We felt unwanted. We'd not been issued with British Expeditionary Force identity cards! Rumours went round that Fifth Columnists dressed in Allied uniforms were sniping in the town. The *gendarmes* were likely to shoot anyone without an ID card. Not wishing to be shot, we lined the rails and watched the colonel engage in a heated argument on the quay with a British officer who had arrived with a car full of baggage, obviously bound for Dover. The colonel had someone dump this on the ground, took over the vehicle, and drove off. We were only allowed ashore when he reappeared, fuming at being refused entry to the French command post. He had to find a British HQ, which had been set up by the port administrative staff.

Threading our way through piles of rations and stores, while avoiding a train pulling in, we headed for the dunes behind the Gare Maritime and sat about. The Queen Victoria's Rifles, who had found some Brens and anti-tank rifles, marched off towards the town. Sirens wailed and we saw black bursts around high-flying bombers. The ack-ack stopped when a couple of fighters appeared and one of the raiders dived into the sea with an almighty splash.

'Serve the bastard right for getting us out of the pub before closing time,' said Socker.

We remained interested spectators until 4 p.m. when the *City of Christchurch* docked: a strange sight, as her decks were stacked with wooden crates.

'Ammunition?'

A seaman enlightened us: 'No. Petrol!'

'Can't be.'

'They're full of four gallon cans, mate.'

In the holds below were our fighting vehicles.

'At least ours should be first off,' said Billy Barlow. 'It was last on.'

Billy was the driver of my scout car. The recce troop had ten Daimler Dingos and was commanded by Lieutenant Morgan. I was his troop sergeant. The Dingo was one of the few vehicles I encountered (on our side) during the war that was ideal for the job it had to do. Less than five feet high, it could travel at 55mph forwards or backwards. It had a crew of two and mounted a single Bren light machine gun. The commander observed from an open cockpit while the No 2 – in my case, Billy – did the driving.

Billy was well known throughout the battalion because his family ran the fish and chip shop at Lydd while we were stationed there during the late 1930s. Although he had been called up as a militiaman before the war, he had managed to get himself posted to us.

The first nagging suspicions that something might be seriously wrong arose as the evening mists closed in. Crate-loads of petrol drums were still piled high on the decks of the *City of Christchurch*. Not unnaturally, the

French dockers, who, in any case, had been working flat out for days and were exhausted, did not want to be cremated alive. Every time the sirens went off, they bolted into shelters. The crew of the *Maid* was not too optimistic about its prospects either and an armed guard was posted to stop any of them clearing off. To make matters worse, the electricity supply to quayside cranes was more frequently off than on, and in the end the ship's derricks had to be used. The sapper unit that had travelled with us worked wonders, but, despite added help from our troopers, the unloading continued at a snail's pace.

As soon as the crews could get into the holds they were down there looking for their machines. Though great care had been taken at Fordingbridge to prepare the tanks for transit according to the regulations – for example, protective mineral jelly had been liberally applied to machine-gun barrels – the *City of Christchurch* had been loaded at Southampton by rule of thumb. The heaviest tanks – thirty cruisers – were in the bottom of the ship, the light tanks on the deck above and the scout cars at the top. The ammunition, spare parts and radio accessories had been tucked away in any odd corner that suited the mate's displacement requirements.

The lighting in the holds was feeble and it did not help matters when it was discovered that in some of the cruisers, which had only recently arrived from the factories, the internal lights were not working. There was an acute shortage of cotton waste, which was needed to clean off the mineral jelly.

Groans of disbelief arose when word went round that most of the .5 rounds for the light tanks were packed loose. Machine-gun ammunition has to be held firmly in its feed belts and a mechanical device is used to force it into the loops. There was no such machine on the ship.

Unable even to enjoy a cigarette because of the fire risk, small groups worked silently in semi-darkness. Most of the noise came from the ship's generators and the men at the derricks. The *City of Christchurch* was no roll-on-roll-off ferry: until the tanks had been hoisted through the hatches and swung ashore they were just so much scrap metal.

Vehicle unloading began in the early hours of the morning. No one got any sleep. I spent much of the time studying the map – one of those collected by the colonel at Dover. I think the CO had been in Calais during the Great War, but to the rest it was unexplored territory. The ground to the north was flat, while the road to the south crossed a ridge on the way to Boulogne. Enemy positions were unknown. The recce troop was ordered to find them when the light improved.

We split into two groups of five vehicles. My troop commander led one up the coast towards Gravelines and Dunkirk. I set off with the other in a southerly direction to search the area around Guines. When we left the battalion, men were sitting in the dunes painfully forcing rounds into ammunition belts, blistering their hands and breaking their nails. Others were cursing ill-fitting machine-gun barrels.

It was another cool misty morning and we got our first close look at Calais as we drove up streets of red-brick houses where bakers were opening their shops. Further on we saw the first refugees, some camping where they had stopped by the roadside and others heading towards the town. We had seen plenty of newsreel scenes of the Spanish Civil War but the haggard looks, the crazy transport – lorries, prams, push carts and bicycles piled high with household goods – were a shock all the same. French soldiers sometimes tramped past, shouting something, but we couldn't stop to find out and wouldn't have understood if we had. Enemy planes flew high overhead and the crowd increased its rate of shuffle.

We drove along the side of a canal part of the way and a few miles out of town the refugees thinned out. With some relief I spotted the first formed body of troops I had seen, vehicles hidden under the trees by the side of the road. They were eating. Some had mess tins in their hands. I signalled to the section to halt and raised my binoculars.

'Oh Christ, Billy, they're Germans! I can see the black crosses on the tanks.'

There was a flash, a bang and something rasped noisily overhead. Another flash, bang and r-r-r-rasp was followed by a solid thump some way behind.

I had been standing – I sat down quickly. The enemy had sited anti-tank guns to cover the road during breakfast.

'Let's get out of here. Quick!'

Bullets cracked on the cobbles, ramming home the personal nature of the affair. I thought: 'My God, it's me they're trying to kill – me!'

This wasn't like random bombing when you might be unlucky. This was an act that had murderous intent. Someone had watched our approach, taken aim through a graduated sight, got us in his cross-wires and pressed the trigger.

Billy remained unruffled. He reversed coolly and deliberately until we were at right angles to the ditch that ran alongside the road, then we bumped over it into a field of half-grown crops.

The two Dingos immediately behind us were doing the same but tipped over, either because they were hit or had taken the ditch at too sharp an angle; they lay there, wheels spinning. No one got out. I could see none of the remaining Dingos.

Fear was now replaced by anger. We had no radio and it was our job to get back as fast as we could and report what we had seen. Then we'd show them.

'Get going, Billy!'

We bumped across the field, with soil flying all around us: the Germans were having no problems with their machine-gun ammunition. A shallow valley offered shelter and we fled up it.

Everyone had been looking for light armoured forces. I reckoned we had found them. But 'light' . . .?

The CO showed obvious irritation when I gave my report, as if I was personally responsible for the loss of two, and possibly four, of 'his' Dingos. To make matters worse, there was no news at all of the rest of the recce troop under Lieutenant Morgan. I was told to stand by and parked near HQ. Regimental Sergeant Major Stannard told me the colonel had every right to be touchy as he was getting a string of contradictory orders. The previous evening he had been confronted by the adjutant general of the BEF, who stopped off at Calais en route for Dover and told him his first priority was to drive to the relief of Boulogne as soon as his tanks were ashore. Later a staff officer arrived with orders for us to take a completely different direction to St Omer where the BEF's main HQ was about to be surrounded. Some light tanks had actually been sent off there.

The adjutant general must have made the greater impression, however, because when the battalion did deploy for action it was at Coquelles on the Boulogne road. The B echelon lorries with our supplies and stores moved into the municipal gardens in the centre of the town.

In the early afternoon we advanced towards Boulogne, my orders being to stick behind the CO's HQ tanks in case I was needed. Once again we drove through crowds of refugees. Half an hour later the leading elements swung off the road to investigate suspicious vehicles beside a wood. One of our troop commanders got to within pistol range before enemy tanks were identified.

It did me good to see our cruisers in action. They were mainly A-13s, racy-looking tanks with four big road wheels on each side and a two-pounder gun for main armament. You could reach 40mph on firm ground. The long days spent on the ranges on the Dorset coast paid off and soon half a dozen German tanks were ablaze. The armour of the A-13s – up to 30mm – seemed able to keep out the enemy shells. Only when the German field guns joined in did the scene change.

The panzers crept nearer and our squadrons began to suffer. One of the A-10s, ugly brutes with box-like turrets and a 3.7-inch mortar instead of a two-pounder, began to burn; a track was blown off another cruiser; and the gun on the colonel's A-13 was shattered. We withdrew over the crest of a ridge and at dusk took up position around a small wood. German bombers flew overhead but ignored us and dumped their cargo on Calais, where the drifting smoke was growing thicker.

About 8 p.m. a staff car appeared from the direction of the town, a senior officer's red band clearly visible. The wearer had a long conversation with the colonel and, when he left, the adjutant, Captain Moss, came over and told me my vehicle had been placed at the disposal of Brigadier Nicholson who had been sent over from England to take overall command at Calais. He had arrived that afternoon but when he tried to raise the colonel on the net, he was told to get off the air as the CO was 'trying to fight a bloody battle'. The colonel had no idea at that time who he was talking to.

We followed the brigadier's car back to Calais. As we pulled away, Billy nodded towards three bundles covered by groundsheets. Boots stuck out from under them.

'Who are they?'

I couldn't say. As they were from tank crews we must both have known them: nearly all of them had been at Lydd.

'What'll happen to them?'

I wasn't sure. We'd never practised burying the dead during exercises on Salisbury Plain.

Chapter Three

Calais: A Token Stand

Brigadier Nicholson was a tall, slim, quietly spoken officer who immediately gave you confidence. Before the war he had commanded the 16th/5th Lancers, taking over the 30th Infantry Brigade in the spring of 1940. They were expecting to provide the motorised element of the 1st Armoured Division when, like us, they were diverted. I had never seen the brigadier until he appeared with his red-banded hat on the Boulogne road.

Two regular battalions, the 1st Rifle Brigade and 1st King's Royal Rifle Corps, had sailed with him after being rushed from East Anglia. Brigade HQ was established in the Boulevard Leon Gambetta in the cellars of a big detached house – a clinic in peacetime – which the previous British senior officer had been using. There was also an HQ section at the Gare Maritime where the navy had a signals link with England.

My task was simple. I had to park the Dingo outside the HQ and wait for orders. That night I drove a short distance down the road to our B echelon in the park, where I left Billy and filled up.

The Parc St Pierre opposite the town hall wasn't a very inspiring place. Lorries had been driven as close to the walls as possible to protect them from blast and splinters, and the drivers and crews from knocked-out tanks were trying to sleep in slit trenches dug into the flower beds. It was bitterly cold.

The park was a good rendezvous but an obvious target and the German gunners had got its range during the day. Every pane had been blown out of the greenhouses and there was the familiar carpet of glass and shattered flower-pots. The bandstand was not going to be much use again that summer. Billy didn't turn a hair at the spectacle but went off to scrounge a couple of mugs of tea.

'So long, sergeant. See you later,' was all he said when I drove off.

Back at the Gare Maritime things were happening. A convoy of ten-tonners was being assembled for a dash up the road to Dunkirk to get some of the mountain of rations on the quayside to the BEF. Half a dozen tanks, part of B Squadron commanded by Major Reeves, were to lead it and a company of the Rifle Brigade was to follow in Bren carriers and lorries. The brigadier wanted to see them off and I drove him down to the start point.

The 'Dunkirk or Bust' party didn't get very far. They ran into anti-tank guns and artillery and after a fierce exchange of fire the whole thing was called off. By then I had driven the brigadier back to his HQ and was sitting in the Dingo again. I had seen for myself enemy tanks east and south of the town and, after the latest encounter, I didn't need Napoleon to tell me that we were surrounded, probably by a panzer division.

Throughout the next day, as the noise of fighting rose and fell and our troops retired to a shorter line, Brigadier Nicholson, still wearing his red band, used the Dingo as a taxi or sent one of his officers in it to visit units. A solitary despatch rider, ready to take messages, accompanied us through the streets, now littered with debris. German bombers seemed to be avoiding the town, which was obscured from the air by the dark clouds over the blazing fuel dumps. Greasy black smuts filled the air.

Having been fought over for hundreds of years by the English and French, there were plenty of ancient strongpoints in Calais. Most were barracks built into stone-faced earthworks. These bastions were numbered in sequence but no longer linked as they had been in the past. Roads and railways had been driven through the original perimeter works. The cornerstone of the defences was still the Citadel, built some 250 years previously by Vauban, the celebrated military engineer. It was roughly the size of a first-class football pitch, surrounded by ramparts and a moat partly filled with water.

French headquarters were in the Citadel, which appeared impervious to the heaviest bombs or shells. Callers were much more likely to fall victim to the nervous sentries on the drawbridge and it was thus one place our (otherwise intrepid) despatch rider approached with the greatest care.

He and I agreed, while waiting by the Dingo, that a built-up area criss-crossed with canals and railway lines was not the ideal place to use a battalion of fast cruiser tanks and a brigade of motorised infantry. There must have been some ghastly mistake at the War Office (we always blamed the War Office for everything). Once they realised what they'd done, we'd be taken out the same way we'd come in – by sea. We took comfort in the news that B echelon of 3RTR had been ordered out of the park to the Gare Maritime to embark for England. Drivers were pushing lorries off the quays into the water so they wouldn't fall into enemy hands. A packed hospital train was cleared and the wounded carried aboard the steamer, *Kohistan*. Men who had died on the journey were left covered in blankets in a row on the platform. Brigadier Nicholson was now mainly operating from the Gare Maritime, which also made sense if we were going to pull out. For me, buoyed by these hopes, the 24th passed quickly. In the early hours of the following morning, however, I was roused and told that HQ was moving to the Citadel.

There was heavy shelling as we drove through the rubble-strewn streets. Overhead cables sagged across the roads.

I was not long at the Citadel. After I'd made a couple of journeys, the brigadier said simply: 'I don't think you can do much more here, sergeant. If you want to try to make it back, it's all right by me.'

Then he added: 'Colonel Keller has no further use for you.'

When I asked about the Dingo he gave a little grin and said: 'I shan't be needing it again.'

I realised something must have happened but couldn't very well ask what. I wished Brigadier Nicholson good luck, saluted and made off. There was no sign of the despatch rider. The brigadier must have realised then that the chances of getting away were fast disappearing. He'd been told on the morning of the 24th that evacuation had been agreed 'in principle' but another signal received late that night said the French were against it. He was told to fight on for the time being.

I knew nothing of these things as I headed for the Gare Maritime. Things had worsened since we left and more burning and abandoned vehicles blocked the roads. The Dingo carried a box of six grenades and

I slipped one of these under the bonnet to set it alight before continuing on foot.

I don't know where the little ship came from or what she was called, and I've wondered since whether she was the trawler mentioned in one account of the battle as having brought an important message for the naval detachment at the Gare Maritime. What I do remember is that they were pulling up the gangplank as I ran down the quayside. Those of us on deck lay flat as we steamed away, to avoid being blown overboard at the last minute. Shells were splashing quite close and once clear of the smoke we could see the flashes of the enemy batteries on the ridge above Coquelles. Destroyers were firing back while zigzagging to avoid the Stukas, which were queuing up to dive on them. Once or twice, ships vanished under clouds of spray but emerged with their pom-poms blazing away.

Near misses blew bits of metal off our superstructure, gashing some of the men, but by mid-Channel the air activity had died down.

Ships from other ports in France had also been landing troops at Dover and the quay was packed. Salvation Army vans were dispensing tea, and ambulances were crawling through the crowds; there were nurses, policemen, redcaps, people pushing chocolate into your hands and giving you cigarettes. No one asked what was happening back there, though the artillery fire could be plainly heard.

I was shoved into a train for Aldershot with a lot of other weary soldiers and, still wearing the revolver I had never drawn, fell fast asleep. I never did get my BEF ID card.

The sergeants' mess reopened in a field at Newbury Park near Cambridge – a marquee, scrubbed tables, chairs folding flat and a couple of borrowed easy chairs. Tiny White, the regimental quartermaster sergeant (RQMS), took over as regimental sergeant major from RSM Stannard, who did make it back, though only after spending a long time in the water after his ship was sunk.

Calais had fallen on 26 May, despite the German command's order that it would be taken on the 25th. Brigadier Nicholson had been captured in the Citadel after refusing a surrender call with the reply: 'The answer is no, as it is the British Army's duty to fight as well as it is the Germans'.'

Now he was on his way to a prisoner-of-war camp in Germany. If he and the men captured with him felt any bitterness about being landed so ill-prepared for their mission, who could blame them? After we'd taken stock, we estimated that out of a war establishment of 575 men of all ranks, slightly more than half had returned, mainly from the B echelon – the fitters, armourers and drivers.

Of the 100 or so men reported killed or missing, most were highly skilled tank crew members, including many troop sergeants. Tubby Ballard was missing – he and I had shared a billet in Hitchin; Ginger May and Tich Kemp, both good friends, were dead; and Socker Heath was thought to have been captured. We'd gone to war on a Tuesday night a regular battalion with fifty tanks, and by Saturday we had lost all our vehicles – tracked and wheeled – and nearly half our strength.

Unpleasant facts came to light. The A-10s might as well have stayed in England. No high-explosive (HE) ammunition had been provided for their mortars and they'd been reduced to firing smoke bombs. With the right ammunition they could have taken on the anti-tank guns that the Germans set up in ruined houses to fire into the thin sides of our cruisers. Solid shot from a two-pounder was useless for this type of target.

At least two tanks had been wrecked by their own crews in full view of everyone near the Gare Maritime on the morning of the 24th when a rumour went round that evacuation was to take place and no serviceable equipment was to fall into enemy hands. More might have been destroyed there and then but someone realised the mistake and called a halt. It was little wonder the French took a sour view of the incident.

Fortunately, there was another side to the coin. The A-13s had destroyed or disabled a number of their opponents. Tank commanders had shown dash when given the opportunity. Major Bill Reeves, sent to scout the road for the 'Dunkirk or Bust' party, had broken through to Gravelines in moonlight and taken part in the defence of the town with his cruiser and three light tanks. Five panzers had been disabled or set on fire. He was awarded an immediate DSO.

My best friend, Jimmy Cornwell, a troop sergeant, also reached Gravelines after devising his own method of clearing a bridge of mines by attaching the tank tow-rope to each of them and dragging them off. Jimmy was decorated with the DCM.

Writing after the war, Sir Basil Liddell-Hart said the operations of 3RTR greatly influenced Hitler's controversial order to halt the panzer divisions along the River Aa instead of letting them advance on Dunkirk. On the 24th the Führer told his generals to leave the destruction of the BEF to the Luftwaffe. The Liddell-Hart theory has been disputed. What seems certain to me is that the garrison of Calais, including all arms of the service, plus the naval gunfire, occupied the full attention of the 10th Panzer Division for three or four days when it might have done considerable mischief elsewhere.

To that extent it may be argued that the heavy losses in men and material were justified, but it was not an argument I cared to use when I went back to Fordingbridge on leave. Most wives were still there. They knew little of where we had been or what we'd been doing. Girls whose husbands were missing kept asking questions we couldn't answer, scrutinising our faces to see if we were concealing anything from them.

Colonel Keller gave us no time to brood. He'd come back via Gravelines after attempting to escape along the beach in a light tank. When it broke down he completed the journey on foot. He'd picked up a bailed-out tank crew on the way but they'd not had the strength to wade across the Aa, which was quite deep near the sea. They'd stayed behind while he pressed on with another officer.

With the threat of invasion hanging over the country, every able-bodied man was involved in defence schemes and, as we had no tanks, we marched about East Anglia carrying Boyes anti-tank rifles: five foot long and hated for their kick and general uselessness.

Gradually we were brought up to strength with replacements from the depot at Bovington and from units that had been to France with the 1st Armoured Division – Bays, 9th Lancers and 10th Hussars. The cavalrymen were all good regular soldiers and quickly settled in as 'tankies', though the absence of machines left us all feeling vulnerable. It was a great relief when we were ordered to hand in the despised Boyes monstrosities and travel to Newmarket to collect a consignment of A-13s and A-15s, all spanking new, the olive-green paint barely dry.

The A-15 was the latest thing in cruisers – similar to, but slightly better protected than the A-13 – and had five road wheels a side instead of four. The main armament was a two-pounder, for which there was still only armour-piercing (AP) shot. The A-15 was later called the Crusader, Mr Churchill feeling keenly that tanks should have names instead of ciphers. One or two old hands reckoned it was a pity he didn't have strong views on supplying HE ammunition.

With the new Dingos came a new commander for the recce troop. Six foot four inches tall and built like the proverbial brick privy, Second Lieutenant Bob Crisp had been commissioned into the Westminster Dragoons, then transferred to 3RTR.

'I hear you play cricket, sergeant.'

'A bit, sir.'

'So do I. We'll have to fix up a net.'

Bob Crisp had taken six wickets in his first test for South Africa against England in 1935.

Cricket was something of an obsession with the peacetime 3RTR. Anyone who as good at it was kept in the battalion. I once had a posting to India cancelled before a vital match. Colonel Keller had played for Hampshire so Bob Crisp could look forward to a rosy future. Within three months he was an acting captain and second-in-command of a squadron.

There was a world of difference between our departure from Dover in May 1940 and our embarkation at Liverpool six months later. The main body of the battalion sailed aboard the liner *Stirling Castle*, which still had a full civilian complement. Some of the older stewards shook their heads at the sight of the lounges and saloons jammed with troopers sleeping head to tail. I shared a cabin with six NCOs but considered it to be preferable to shivering in a hut behind barbed wire in north Germany, where I learned Socker Heath had finished up. The tanks, repainted a sandy colour, travelled on two fast Glen Line steamers accompanied by skeleton crews. We left the Dingos behind.

No one was allowed ashore when the convoy put into Freetown, Sierra

Leone for twenty-four hours, but at Durban we were given local leave. People were queuing at the docks to take us to their homes and we had four wonderful days. The cabin staff of the liner must have enjoyed themselves too, for, when we sailed, many of them failed to report and we finished the voyage carrying out their duties for them.

Bob Crisp also missed the boat. He'd been a reporter on the *Natal Mercury* before the war and been given a riotous welcome by his former colleagues. It must have been a good party because a major and a couple of senior captains missed the boat with him. I don't know whether the CO was pleased or not when one of the cruisers escorting us signalled that she had the absentees on board. They were transferred to us at sea and the 'Demon Bowler' landed at Port Said as plain Second Lieutenant Crisp again.

Our arrival was not impressive. No one sang 'Bless 'em all'. A train was waiting to meet the boat but when it pulled into El Amariya near Alexandria, no arrangements had been made to receive us. An Australian infantry battalion took pity and let us share its camp – officers in their officers' mess, sergeants in their sergeants' mess and so on. It was Christmas Eve, 1940.

The next day our benefactors gave us a splendid Christmas dinner and we all went to one of Shafto's open-air cinemas. The Aussies didn't think much of the film and set the place on fire. We trooped out and sat in the sand drinking Tooth's Lager and watching the cinema burn down. Mr Shafto was reputed to be very rich with many cinemas so he didn't get much sympathy!

A new formation was created, the 2nd Armoured Division, of which 3RTR was a part. We joined the division after a pleasant journey by rail along the coast to Mersa Matruh. Shortly afterwards we would be returning to the delta.

'What's up?'

'We've got to hand over our tanks to the 2nd Battalion.'

'I don't believe it.'

'It's true.'

'And what are we going to use?'

'It's a swap.'

'Roll on.'

We were being asked to exchange our fine new cruisers for five-year-old machines, which had already covered hundreds of miles. Recce was also to hand over the light tanks we'd been given in place of the Dingos. Bitter words were spoken when the exchange took place. Even more colourful views on the competence of the Staff were expressed when we loaded up the worn-out A-10s and set off back to the delta. We were mystified.

In camp again near Alexandria we were called together in squadrons and learned our fate. We were to become part of the 1st Armoured Brigade bound for Greece.

'What about spares, sir?' the squadron leader was asked.

'They're being sent out.'

It was nice to know. The A-10 had good articulated suspension but needed expert attention to keep it going over long distances. Those handed over by 2RTR had two-pounders instead of the mortars we had used at Calais but they didn't make up for the weak armour. The Italian M13/40 was better protected and its 47mm gun was heavier. What was more, we would be lucky if the M13/40 was the only opponent we met. Mussolini's troops had been having a hard time of it after attacking Greece in October 1940 and it was a reasonable assumption that Hitler would intervene. Otherwise, why were we being sent out? No one had any illusions about what would happen if we came up against German Mark IIIs and IVs.

The only other armoured unit going out, the 4th Hussars, was equipped with Mark VIBs, armed with machine guns only – a .303 medium and a .5 heavy. They were fast but their armour was only 13mm thick.

It seemed there was little time to lose. At the beginning of March we boarded the new anti-aircraft cruiser *Bonaventure* and steamed through the Mediterranean at high speed in the company of the older cruisers *Gloucester* and *York*. Within thirty-six hours we were in Piraeus. The Greeks went wild with delight and hung garlands round our necks. When the unloved A-10s arrived by fast freighter a couple of days later they decorated them with flowers.

For two days we sat around the harbour in Piraeus awaiting the arrival of our tanks. I took the opportunity of going into Athens and in a small cafe was lucky enough to meet a Greek schoolteacher who spoke English and indeed taught English in his school. He invited me to his house and I met his wife and two daughters. This opportune encounter was to help me considerably later on.

Chapter Four

A Greek Interlude, Part I

The A-10s and the Greek rolling stock at least had something in common: both were clapped out and lacked essential bits and pieces. The flat-cars carrying the tanks to the front were seriously lacking in chains to hold their loads in position. As substitutes we bolted strong planks to the wagon floors to act as chocks.

The crews, someone decided, would travel on the same transport as their vehicles. There was to be no question of the two becoming separated. Tarpaulin shelters were rigged up behind the tanks but the structures looked so precarious I was glad I was going by road. I had been promoted squadron quartermaster sergeant and my transport consisted of a fifteen-hundredweight truck and a three-ton lorry.

The job of the QMS was to ensure the squadron was supplied with ammunition, rations and personal requisites such as toothpaste and cigarettes. I can't say I was mad about it as the previous time I'd carried out similar duties as battalion ration sergeant I ran into trouble by ordering too many turkeys. At Christmas 1939, the bill was more than £100 over the allowance, an enormous sum in those days, though somehow it was fielded by the quartermaster, Captain Reggie de Vere. However, when the men were served half a kipper each one morning – no one had told me you ordered them in pairs – he gave me up in disgust. For some time afterwards I was known as 'Half Kipper Close'.

Shortly before we left Athens, the battalion changed out of khaki drill and shorts, back into battledress. The weather, which had been warm and pleasant when we set up camp under the trees in the Glades of Daphne, was changing. We were warned to expect snow in the north, where we were bound. As we pulled out, sola topees, supplied by a thoughtful government, stood abandoned in neat rows.

The forecasters had made no mistake. Our convoy was met in the mountains by flurries of sleet, which sometimes developed into minor blizzards. Windscreen wipers worked overtime. The further we drove, the wilder the scenery became – jagged cliffs towered on one side while scree fell sharply on the other. Snow-covered peaks appeared during breaks in the cloud but the valleys were wreathed in gloom and mist. It didn't look like good tank country to me. It didn't look like good country for anything much at all.

It took us three days to reach Florina, the railhead for the Greek armies fighting in Albania. There the tank crews rejoined us with hair-raising tales. They'd nearly frozen to death the first day as the engine driver had no idea of the importance of tea to the average tankie and they'd been unable to brew up on the windswept flat-cars. At the first stop a delegation repaired this gap in the driver's education and from then on there were regular stops to draw boiling water from the locomotive.

'It's a miracle we weren't all killed' was a phrase I heard repeatedly. Some tanks had slipped an inch or two when the flat-cars rounded steep bends. As hail and ice built up under the tracks there were fears the fifteen-ton A-10s would slither over the chocks and carry away the half-frozen crews with them. Even after all these years it still seems to me to have been a lunatic way to risk the cream of an armoured regiment. However, they got there, though one wondered how.

Florina was a largish, dilapidated town full of soldiers, shopkeepers, pot-holed streets and little cafes. The battalion trekked almost immediately to Amyntaio, a smaller and dirtier version of Florina. Colonel Keller set up his headquarters in the schoolhouse, the vehicles were dispersed around it and camouflaged, and the squadrons took up position. Students of the use of armour will look in vain for any virtue in these positions. The tanks had to crawl over rutted trails, sometimes waterlogged, sometimes frozen iron-hard, to isolated locations covering the approach roads. There was little prospect of mutual support. The low ground was a morass, generally impassable, and even the better valleys could not be crossed unless a route was reconnoitred and marked out immediately beforehand. At night temperatures nose-dived and the crews, for the most part, bivouacked in snow holes alongside the A-10s.

Given good artillery and air cover, determined troops could expect to hold up an invader in the mountains indefinitely as long as he was obliging enough to commit himself to a frontal assault. There was, however, no telling from which direction the enemy might arrive. When we arrived at Amyntaio the Germans had still not shown their hand. The Greeks were heavily engaged in Albania – and not having it all their own way by any means – while a variety of rumours was coming out of Yugoslavia.

Unable to make head nor tail of Balkan politics, the average tankie tried to keep himself warm and looked forward to going out on patrols if only because they broke the monotonous mountain vigil. Inter-squadron football matches were arranged and a game against a Greek anti-aircraft battery took on the importance of a cup final. News of the arrival of the spare parts for the tanks was nothing short of sensational.

The squadron's quartermaster sergeants immediately drove down to the sidings at Florina to load up. We were desperately short of spare links and were patching up old tracks as best we could. A few packing cases were opened before the full horror dawned.

'Look at this, Q.'

The technical adjutant had come down with us. He held up a well-greased track pin.

'They've sent us the bloody spares for A-15s and A-13s!'

Talk about a stunned silence.

'The 2nd Tanks are going to be pleased when they get our junk,' someone said.

'Blow the 2nd Tanks. There must be other spares for A-15s around in Egypt. What are we going to do now?'

There was nothing to be done. I went off to see if I could arrange any business with the Royal Army Service Corps (RASC) field supply depot, where we had some good friends. We could usually scrounge a chest of tea or a sack of sugar if the storemen conspired to distract their own RQMS when we were stacking up.

No one ever checked the loaded lorries. Perhaps that was what had happened to our tank parts . . . nobody checked. When the Germans attacked Greece and Yugoslavia with seven panzer divisions on 6 April we had plenty of tea and sugar but no spare A-10 track plates.

The condition of stragglers retiring through Amyntaio told its own story. Mud-covered Greek soldiers trudged through the uneven streets. Refugees crowded the road into Florina. Drenching rain and low clouds added to the misery but at least kept the Stukas away. Then the weather improved and the bombing started. Our squadrons reported contact with the enemy.

For three days the battalion and the 4th Hussars were involved in the shambles known as the battle of the Monastir Gap, along with Australian infantry, New Zealand machine-gunners and Northumberland Hussars – anti-tank gunners, despite their title.

I spent my time taking up supplies to the squadron, sometimes bringing back crews from damaged tanks. The lack of spares was now telling. One squadron reported five breakdowns alone while investigating what turned out to be a false alarm. All the machines had to be abandoned and destroyed. There were no means of recovering them.

Quite a number of enemy armoured vehicles were knocked out or damaged but unlike ours, theirs were soon repaired. With the surrender of the Greek army in Macedonia, our rear was threatened and retreat became inevitable.

The distance involved, 300 miles or so to Thermopylae, was too much for the worn tracks of the A-10s. Our strength wasted away on the mountain roads. What might have been achieved under different circumstances was shown at Ptolemaida, forty miles south of our original position. Supported by anti-tank gunners and twenty-five-pounders, C Squadron set up an ambush covering the bridge. The Germans drove right into it and a number of panzer IIIs went up in flames together with some half-tracks. Unfortunately, three more of our tanks were reduced to a state beyond repair.

Bob Crisp came into his own during the retreat. At the mountain village of Grevena he found a good position, camouflaged his tank, and used his machine guns on the Messerschmitts and Stukas flying up the valleys. When the battalion reached Larissa, where the Greeks had their main headquarters and supply depots, he fought a final battle on the airfield amid the burnt-out Hurricanes which had been caught on the ground. After that there was virtually nothing left to fight with. The only tanks we had left were on our cap badges.

'All right, Q. The orders are simple. We drive back to Athens, catch the train for Argos, find T Beach and wait for the navy. Got it?'

'Got it, sir!'

Captain Bartrum, who was in charge of the transport, was standing in the slush of a dismal village just outside Larissa. Lined up in the main street were fourteen three-tonners and my own fifteen-hundredweight truck. The lorries were full of weary tankies, two or three young troop officers, bailed-out crews and echelon personnel, about 250 in all.

They huddled on piles of bedrolls, stores and boxes of ammunition. A number of Besas had been extracted from the tanks and mounted on top of the cabs of the Bedfords. We devised a system by which one man acted as observer/loader while the other fired the gun. It was only a matter of time before the Luftwaffe started to fly from Larissa.

We started in good order across the plain and headed for the mountains, lorries at reasonable distances. As we got into the foothills and joined the hordes of other travellers it became more and more difficult to maintain convoy discipline.

We were submerged in a slow-moving stream of people and vehicles, on which the enemy planes swooped at will. The peasants, Greeks and Turks, were unbelievably poor, though most hospitable, and were determined to leave nothing behind. They crammed their worldly goods, children and relatives onto any available transport and abandoned their farms and villages.

Winding along the sides of the mountains, through the passes over precarious bridges, we trekked amid files of worn-out Greek infantry in khaki and puttees, cannon and limbers pulled by shaggy ponies, ambulances, buses, ox-carts, cattle, mules and donkeys – plenty of mules and donkeys.

When the German fighters came streaking up the valleys with their cannons blazing, the column shuddered to a halt and people threw themselves into a ditch – if there was one handy – or cowered behind the boulders on the mountain-side. When the planes had gone, disabled or burning vehicles were pushed aside and sent tumbling down the slopes, the wounded were bandaged and, when it was possible, graves scraped for the dead. The human snake reformed, jerked into motion and went on until the planes appeared again. One afternoon Stukas attacked every half hour. Two of our lorries went up in smoke and their passengers crowded onto the remaining vehicles. The dead, minus their payrolls taken for identification purposes, were rolled in groundsheets and left by the roadside.

Over a period of some three days and nights the horror – burning villages, and dead civilians outnumbering dead soldiers – became commonplace. About thirty miles from Thermopylae a great cheer went up as we parked near some bubbling warm springs. Filthy from jumping in and out of ditches, we stripped off and steeped our aching limbs. Then the Stukas appeared again. The pilots must have had a clear view of our pink bodies as we headed once more for the nearest mud holes.

At Thermopylae, where a stand was to be made, we were waved through the defences – tank crews were not needed. Due to silting up, the famous old battlefield was no longer a narrow pass but had become a broad plain between the hills and the sea. We made good speed on the road to Athens after we left Thermopylae, though the convoy became more and more extended. This created problems at roadblocks. Not far from the city, heavily armed Greeks on the look-out for German parachutists, stared suspiciously at the machine guns on the cabs of the Bedfords and even harder at the grimy figures manning them.

Captain Bartrum, who had done everything humanly possible to keep the convoy together, had to give a lengthy explanation. Finally he called me over.

'Q, you'd better stay and direct the drivers as they arrive. Send them up that road there.'

We were at a roundabout with a number of exits.

'What about the fifteen-hundredweight, sir?'

'I'll go ahead in it and see what's going on at the station. You'd better catch the last lorry in. You'll be able to find us all right.'

'Don't worry about me, sir.' I sounded more optimistic then I felt.

No old soldier ever trusts his kit to anyone else. I went over to the truck and collected my haversack. Apart from containing my razor, it was stuffed with Greek drachmae: I had been about to deliver the squadron pay when the retreat started.

I slung the satchel over my shoulder and waited. The fifteen-hundred-weight went off with the few lorries that had already arrived and I checked in the laggards who came in at longer and longer intervals. The 'last' vehicle was 'not far behind' I was told. It would be with me 'in ten minutes'.

The ten minutes became fifteen . . . thirty . . . an hour. I became conscious of the strange looks I was getting from passing Greeks. Some of them looked enviously at the pistol strapped to my side.

It was a long walk into the city. No one stopped to give me a lift. The days of garlands and free drinks had gone.

There were Greek sentries at the first station I went to and they wouldn't let me in. They made out they didn't understand me and waved me away to try elsewhere. I tramped on for what seemed to be miles and found another station. In my khaki cardigan, battledress trousers and black tank beret I couldn't have been anything else but a British soldier, yet no one wanted to know.

A Greek with a rifle and bayonet sent me on my way. The few people about averted their eyes in the streets. Police patrols frequently stopped and questioned me at gunpoint. If the Germans were regarded as the hated enemy, I gathered that the British were not universally popular either.

As I knew only one private house in Athens I decided to try my luck there. Andrei, the schoolmaster who taught English, had been among the first to welcome us when we arrived. I had spent two days with him and his family on weekend leave in Athens. Tall and fair, he didn't look at all like my idea of a Greek. I wondered whether I would still be welcome — if I could find the way to his house.

I tracked him down with some difficulty. He happened to be at home and the moment I knocked, he hauled me inside and shut the door quickly.

'What are you doing here? How did you find us? The radio says the Germans are already here. The government has capitulated.' I felt a bit like I did when I told Colonel Keller I had lost my Dingo section. It was all my fault.

Chapter Five

A Greek Interlude, Part II

The red-light district in Athens was probably the best-informed commercial centre in the Balkans. All the pimps were spies, all the girls reported interesting pillow-talk to madame, and every client had a tale to tell. Thanks to some Australians, I ended up there in a rather luxurious establishment. I met the Aussies in a cafe when, wearing one of Andrei's jackets over my battledress trousers, I carried out a little recce one evening after dark. They were sitting in their shirtsleeves cheerfully drinking beer and swapping yarns.

'There's nothing wrong with our hide-out,' one of them explained, 'but you can have too much of a good thing.'

They invited me to move in with them and, after consulting Andrei, I did. I couldn't see myself spending the rest of the war helping his teenage daughters practise their English. Furthermore, once the Germans got a real grip on the city any Athenian sheltering a British soldier would be in trouble.

The brothel was well supplied with plush armchairs, heavy curtains and dim lights. We spent most of our time sitting about the heavily perfumed lounge talking to the girls hanging about the bar. They were very sympathetic and nearly all spoke some English.

I heard a number of things. First, that Captain Bartrum's convoy of tankies had made the train and gone off to Argos; the Greek prime minister had committed suicide, though the Germans said the Allies had shot him; Nazi paratroops had dropped on the only bridge spanning the Corinth Canal and captured it after a fierce battle with the New Zealanders.

Someone had then blown it up, and a lot of enemy soldiers with it.

The navy was still picking up people off the beaches on the

Peloponnese peninsula, it was rumoured, but the 2nd Panzer Division had occupied the area around Athens.

Most interesting of all was a report that British troops were gathering at Glyfada – a well-known beauty spot – where a mysterious one-eyed major was organising escape parties in the woods.

Madame, a smartly dressed woman of about forty who would have made a success of any business, arranged things for us. One night a pimp brought news that we were to walk to Glyfada after dark and we duly did so, though it was quite a step.

Our trust in the lady was completely justified. To my surprise, the one-eyed officer – whom the old desert hands had immediately dubbed 'Wahid Shufti' behind his back – was wearing a black beret. It was Major Carey, second-in-command of 3RTR, who had been sent on ahead to liaise with the Greeks for our entry into Greece. In any case, Major Carey knew his stuff, saying he didn't want anyone to end up as he had done in the Great War – a prisoner. He must have gathered more than fifty soldiers there, most of whom had been sleeping rough in the woods. Some were in full battle order with small packs, pouches and rifles, and some were unarmed, with not much more than an overcoat. There were quite a few tankies among them, including John Myers, a particular friend who had served with me when the battalion was at Lydd.

The major wasted no time in forming us into parties to attempt an escape across the Corinth Canal and head for the southern beaches. One or two people had maps of the area already and the rest copied them. We also made crude sketches of Crete – which we were to head for if we were lucky. As I had a prismatic compass, a map and my supply of cash, Major Carey put me in charge of about a dozen men, most of whom were armed. Then he introduced me to George, a dark, wiry Greek lad of about fifteen who was to be our guide. George spoke some English and had already taken at least one party across the canal.

The drill was to move along the roads at night, taking to the fields if we saw headlights, which the Germans, not being worried about air attacks, used freely. It was estimated that it would take three nights to reach the crossing place on the canal.

We walked until nearly dawn when, somewhere behind the sprawling suburbs of Eleusis, we climbed a steep hill to a monastery where the monks seemed to have been expecting us. They fed us, gave us hot tea and goat's milk and let us sleep in the crypt. At dusk, when we were roused and given bread and tomatoes, we learned that German patrols had passed through the area without stopping.

On the next stage of the journey we must have covered twenty miles in the direction of Megara. It was a cold, misty night and once or twice the glare of headlights forced us to take to the fields. We couldn't see what the vehicles were and weren't concerned to find out. Daybreak saw us at a friendly farm where we were glad of the hot coffee the owner provided. We hid in a barn all day and watched German half-tracks and armoured cars drive past on the road below. When we left, I dipped into the squadron's imprest account to pay for the food we had eaten. The farmer protested but took it in the end. The generosity of the desperately poor peasants in country areas made a lasting impression.

We had hoped to reach the canal the next night but were still on the road when the sky began to lighten. George led us into the hills and we lay sweltering under some stunted olive trees all day. After dark we made good progress and reached the rocky slopes bordering the canal comparatively quickly.

It ran dead straight in both directions. I learned much later that when the Romans ruled Greece Emperor Nero had encouraged the digging of the first practical cutting – before then people used to drag ships from one gulf to another. All I could think of at the time was that it looked very wide and was probably pretty deep. The sides were almost sheer and it seemed impossible that we could negotiate them at night with German sentries at intervals along the top.

However, we were successful and, saying goodbye to George with a generous handful of my drachmae to help him on his way back to Athens, we made our way further south.

Looking back, I sometimes wonder if the Germans were quite happy to leave us to our own devices. They could have wasted a lot of petrol chasing us round the mountains and must have realised that a sweep of the beaches would round up most stragglers later.

As we continued our journey in the same fashion, moving by night and lying up by day, we came across dozens of similar parties, all hoping to be picked up by the navy. The hills were alive after dark. Near the coast we fell in with a party of about 300 men, with a variety of cap badges, under the command of a middle-aged gunner major. When I reported to him he told me to join his group and said gloomily that the enemy was already at Argos rounding up thousands of troops who had reached the beaches on the coast beyond.

'What will you do, sir?'

'There's nothing else to be done. I intend to surrender tomorrow. We can't fight and we can't run. We'll simply go into the bag in an orderly fashion. See your men hand in their weapons.' And he mentioned some arrangement he had made to collect them.

I took the good news back to my little squad. Nobody cheered.

'I don't think this is what Wahid Shufti had in mind,' said one of the Aussies.

They all stared hard at me.

'What do you think, Q?'

'Well, I don't know for certain what I'm going to do, but I'm not staying here.'

'Where will you go?'

'Back into the hills and try to get round Argos further along the coast.'

Only two of my original party decided they'd had enough. They were exhausted – at least as far as their morale was concerned. The rest of us, six from 3RTR (including John Myers and myself), two Australians, two New Zealanders and a Royal Engineers corporal, slipped away at dusk.

We spent another four or five days living rough and keeping to the heights. When we stopped we took it in turn to mount guard. When we walked someone scouted ahead. According to my map there was a small fishing community between Argos and Paraliou Astrous and that was where we made for. The peasants we met en route were all sympathetic, though they usually took us to the village priest – most of whom had a smattering of English – to be vetted. Once he said we were all right we were given food and a hiding place. I used some of my drachmae to buy blocks of bitter black chocolate to nibble while we were lying up. The sapper corporal said it was the only thing that put him off escaping.

The village must have had a name but I never found out what it was. There were only half a dozen houses, a harbour wall and an ancient stone jetty sheltering it from the sea. Three or four fishing boats were tied up at the quayside, crab pots on their decks. In the early evening, when we felt certain it was safe, I went down to make contact. A woman in a head-scarf and shawl came out of a door, saw me and quickly went in again. Soon afterwards a young man emerged. The woman watched from the window. From my dishevelled state it must have been clear that I was no German.

For once, no priest appeared; he may have been away. In his place, I was led to a sort of 'head man', a thick-set, unshaven individual of about sixty who occupied pride of place in a room lit by oil lamps that was a cross between a kitchen and a cafe. Hands were shaken all round and the rest of the squad, less the sentries, joined us. Small cups of coffee were placed on a big table.

I would love to have known what the conversation was really about. The man's understandable vocabulary was limited to 'OK', 'No OK', 'Germani' – spit and a thumb across his throat – and 'Mussolini' – a flash of the eyes and a veritable slash across his windpipe.

I did my best to indicate not only that I needed the use of a boat but that I was prepared to hire one. Out of my haversack I produced a bundle of notes. This made a considerable impression.

After a long, garbled discussion, we eventually reached an agreement. The fisherman would be paid so much when we set off and the balance on reaching Khania on Crete, which I pointed out on one of the crude maps drawn up in the woods at Glyfada. We would also pay for the supplies we might need. Once the deal had been reached we got to work stocking the boat with cans of water, bread and the inevitable tomatoes, and the following morning, about 4.30 a.m., chugged out in thick mist. Our skipper seemed to have no navigational aids so I made a brave show of studying my prismatic compass and home-made map. He took no notice.

About three miles offshore a long grey shape slid out of the fog. There was an awful moment of waiting, then a voice boomed across the swell: 'Ahoy there, fishing boat. Stand by to be picked up.'

Scrambling nets were lowered and the boatman was still counting his final pay-off as we clambered aboard the destroyer.

'You were lucky, mate,' said one of the crowd of soldiers hanging over the side. He was right. The fishing boat was barely visible at a few yards in the fog.

HMS *Hotspur*, carrying about 300 escapees like ourselves, was bound for Crete and then Egypt, we were told. All being well, we would be landed at Alexandria. Unhappily, when the sun burnt off the sea mist, Stukas appeared. Everyone lay flat and hung on as the *Hotspur* heeled over, zigzagging to avoid the diving aircraft. Tons of water cascaded over us from near misses. The concussion lifted us bodily and slammed us back on the deck. A hollow clang above the roar of the ack-ack guns told us we'd been hit but the *Hotspur* steamed on. After another resounding crash our speed fell dramatically. It was announced over the tannoy system that the engine room had been damaged but that *Hotspur* could still steam. Instead of going to Alexandria, however, we would be disembarked on Crete. The Stukas flew away and, with the coast in sight, boats and life-rafts were cleared for launching. We were being ferried to the beach when the Stukas reappeared and more bombs thundered around the *Hotspur*. She carried on out to sea, gathering speed slightly but on fire and listing badly. All her guns were in action.

Setting foot on Crete wasn't the most reassuring experience, even though it was clearly a much healthier place that the deck of the *Hotspur*. Intent on destroying her, the Stukas flew off, leaving us on a deserted beach. There was no sign of habitation, just a hinterland of grey-green mountains under a clear blue sky – picture postcard stuff. The idyllic atmosphere was too much for some of the more exhausted troops, who threw them-selves down in the dunes and slept. No one emerged from the crowd to take charge and there was a lot of aimless wandering about. After about forty-eight hours, during which there was intense air activity, we were challenged by a patrol of the Black Watch, who subsequently called up a couple of three-tonners to collect us. At Khania we cleaned ourselves up, had a hot meal, drew blankets and were allotted billets in a large building.

One thing we were desperately anxious for was news of the general situation and the Black Watch sensibly realised this. An officer briefed us about the Greek capitulation and the withdrawal of the British and Commonwealth forces. Most of them, he said, had got away, but the Germans were not expected to be content with their victory on the mainland and an invasion of Crete was imminent.

'You will all be issued with rifles and come under command,' he concluded. 'You, Q, will be in command of a section.'

From their faces, the tankies present – myself included – didn't think much of the idea.

'Can't be helped, chaps,' said the Jock officer. 'We need everyone we can get to patrol this place.'

I asked if there were any tanks on the island and whether it would be possible to join them. He said there was a squadron of the 3rd Hussars with light tanks at the other end of Crete and half a dozen Matildas split up among the airfields. That was all. He didn't know of any replacements or spare machines. We went off to collect our rifles.

For a couple of days we carried out patrols with the Highlanders, searching for parachutists who were reported to have landed. Fortunately we didn't find any, though we saw plenty of the Luftwaffe. Then came news of a serious setback in the desert. A German tank force that had arrived to help out the Italians had not only driven the British back from El Agheila – they'd been doing that when we first arrived in Greece – but had pushed us back to the Egyptian border. The 9th Australian Division was besieged in Tobruk and the 2nd Armoured Division, to which we had originally been assigned, had been badly mauled. All trained tank crews were to be sent back to Egypt as quickly as possible.

We handed back our rifles without regret and climbed aboard lorries sent to take us to a small bay near Suda Bay, where a ship was said to be waiting.

Any sense of deliverance vanished long before we got there. The anchorage was under furious air attack. Two destroyers appeared to be on fire and a cruiser was listing badly. There were no signs of aerial opposition to the howling Stukas.

'You lot tankies?'

48

An officer appeared.

'You're to report to . . .' and he gave the name of some place which turned out to be an inlet along the coast. 'I'd be quick about it if I were you.'

The *Popeii Veronica* was moored in a little cove, her dirty white hull dappled with rust. She didn't show any sign of life apart from some washing hanging near the stern. If the German aircraft ignored her it was possibly because they thought she was a fixture. She'd been laid up for a year and her main function was to provide a home for her owner, his wife and their teenage daughter. The skipper was a giant of a man with a thick black beard and he didn't give much for our chances of getting away. The '*Poppy*' had boiler trouble, engine trouble, condenser trouble . . .

The RASC captain in charge of our party asked the tank fitters if they could do anything, and, inspired by the renewed sound and fury issuing from Suda, volunteers disappeared below decks. Being the only 'Q' on board, I was told to organise the rations for a three-day voyage. 'Blackbeard', who spoke some English, warned me that his fresh-water tanks were leaking or empty, so I scrounged as many empty petrol cans as I could ashore and filled them at a standpipe. These were ferried laboriously aboard the *Veronica*, along with cases of bully, biscuits and cheese from a pile of rations on the quay.

Everybody was allotted a task and some gunners rigged up an ingenious mounting so that they could fire their Besas – taken from broken-down tanks – from a taut wire hawser. One of the 3RTR corporals, Jock Ogilive, who had come out of Greece in a fishing smack manned by the Royal Navy, had refused an order to throw his machine gun overboard, saying he hadn't brought it hundreds of miles to chuck it in the sea, especially as there was a box of ammunition to go with it.

The clanks and bangs from the engine room eventually bore fruit. One of the *Veronica*'s two boilers was declared serviceable. Wisps of black smoke rose from the funnel. I think Blackbeard managed to shanghai a couple of real stokers or engineers from somewhere to show what should be done and the tankies were then split into shifts to fire the solitary boiler.

49

The bunkers were fairly low and soon, with everyone scratching around for coal, there was a film of black dust everywhere.

Gradually the steam pressure built up, until Blackbeard declared, rather to his own amazement, that we could set sail. We watched anxiously as the suspect winch heaved in the anchor chain and at twilight, with the skipper on the bridge, headed out with a destroyer as escort. Goodbye Suda Bay – goodbye Crete. The black gangs worked with a will all night; soldiers were posted round the ship as look-outs.

A beautiful dawn was marred only by the dark line of Crete's cliffs, still barely visible. A glance over the *Poppy*'s side showed barely a ripple on the glassy sea. She was under way, but only just. As the light improved the first German aircraft flew over towards Suda and soon violent noises were again echoing across the water. Our escorting destroyer, which had been describing all sorts of manoeuvres to keep station with us, finally gave up, signalled 'Goodbye and good luck' and, gathering speed, steamed off to join in the mayhem up the coast.

The *Poppy* seemed loath to leave her cosy anchorage but gradually Crete fell behind. While the propeller kept up a slow chunk-chunk-chunking, Blackbeard was happy; but he insisted that three-and-a-half knots was the limit for his crippled engine. From time to time an enthusiastic shift would pile on the fuel until the old tub began to throb, showering us with flakes of paint, but it never lasted long, which was probably just as well. One result of this snail's pace, however, meant that the voyage was going to take longer than expected and I organised things so that we made tea twice a day, the stoking parties getting a mug per man, the rest of us half a mug per brew. The daily food allocation was half a tin of bully, one packet of biscuits and half a pat of cheese per person.

On the second night out, I was standing yarning with John Myers about the good old days before the war when the sea, quite placid up to then, started to foam in the moonlight a few hundred yards away. The deck was crowded and all chatter ceased as a submarine emerged and lay silhouetted on the surface. Some brave soul cocked one of the Besas but a voice in plain English broke the tension:

'Heave to, what ship are you? Where are you bound?'

Blackbeard left it to our RASC captain to explain that if we stopped we might never get going again and that we were British soldiers bound for Egypt. The submarine checked our course, told us were headed in the right direction and accompanied us for the rest of the night, no doubt charging her batteries. Before dawn she submerged, her captain promising to keep an eye on us.

More sinister visitors arrived the next day, a line of twin-engine aircraft flying low over the horizon. One of them broke away to look us over and then called in its friends. For a few minutes there were JU-88s roaring in from all angles, machine guns snarling – ours and theirs – and spray flying. Just as quickly, the Junkers formed single file again and went on their way, leaving the *Poppy* chugging through a lather of foam. They must have completed a bombing mission and used us for target practice on their way back to base. No one was hurt but Blackbeard was outraged and rose from behind the bridge rail where he had been lying, cursing furiously. Mrs Blackbeard, who had hardly been seen since we put to sea, also appeared to hurl shrill abuse after the departing planes and to take in her washing. Other planes attacked us from time to time but our capacity to make an impressive amount of smoke while almost standing still deceived them all and only a couple of cannon shells from marauding Messerschmitts hit the ship without doing any harm.

Though the enemy failed to stop us, it began to look as though we would drift to a halt for want of fuel. The coal was almost gone. We passed on this information to the submarine, which reappeared after dark, and told her captain that if he noticed anything different about our appearance it would be because we were going to burn the deckhouse. And we did – plus various hatch covers and cabin fittings, until finally we started on the deck planking, which had once been caulked and, the stokers told me, 'burned beautifully'. With dignified resignation, Blackbeard accepted the dismantling of his vessel as inevitable. He remained calm so long as we did not push his engines beyond three-and-a-half knots.

With the Egyptian coast in sight our submarine surfaced in daylight and led us towards Alexandria where a tug had been ordered to meet us. Sirens shrieked and foghorns greeted us as we limped in, our giant captain (surrounded by his family) standing in a heroic posture on the bridge.

Quite a reception had been laid on, including doctors and nurses for one or two wounded we were carrying, and after a hot bath and a change of clothes we were given a magnificent meal in one of the city's best hotels. Then transport took us to our units.

What was left of 3RTR was at Heliopolis, guarding the airfield. There I learned that Captain Bartrum and the convoy of lorries had been captured to a man after reaching Argos, while the CO and all the squadron leaders had made it back without ever touching Crete. To me and some of the others who had taken the 'scenic route' back, it didn't seem to be right at all.

Chapter Six

A Time for Reorganisation

It was a new-look battalion that took up residence at Beni Yusef, a collection of sun-baked tents and huts on the Sweet Water Canal about twenty miles from Cairo. When we moved out from Heliopolis at the end of August 1941 we had changed our commanding officer, acquired a different regimental sergeant major, and been equipped with a new tank.

The previous CO, Colonel Keller, went onto the Staff and handed over to Lieutenant Colonel 'Bunny' Ewins, a cavalryman; Paddy Hehir, the regimental quartermaster sergeant who had been with 3RTR since before the war, became RSM in place of Tiny White, who had been captured in Greece; and we got the American M3 light tank, the General Stuart. Also new was the DSO ribbon on Captain Crisp's tunic, awarded for his gallant exploits in Greece. He became commander of C Squadron.

For myself there was promotion to squadron sergeant major – I sported a crown on a leather wrist strap – and I joined B Squadron under Major George Witheridge. He and I had both been in the sergeant's mess at Warminster in 1938.

The reorganisation of the battalion occupied all our attention. Men sent to us from the Royal Armoured Corps pool in the delta belonged to a variety of regiments; for example, there were quite a few 8th Hussars among them. They had to be made welcome and given confidence, not an automatic thing when it was on the record that 3RTR had lost every tank, every vehicle and at least half its personnel in both the campaigns in which it had been engaged. The British regimental system is tried and tested but concentrates on drumming into a recruit that his own outfit (and its traditions) is the best. Having to learn to handle a tank that was completely new to everyone helped the shaking-down process. It gave us a common bond.

Bob Crisp has always claimed that the Stuart got its nickname from a remark made by his driver when he first tried it out in the desert. After putting it through its paces he exclaimed, 'It's a honey,' and the name stuck. Certainly it was ideally suited to the role for which it was originally intended – reconnaissance. It was fast, with an official top speed of 35mph, though it could beat that over good ground. Its radial aircraft engine was first class and needed minimal attention.

Revolutionary as far as we were concerned were the track links mounted in solid rubber blocks. They appeared to be practical and we would find out for sure in due course. American instructors who briefed us on the 'Honeys' swore by their mechanical reliability and we were inclined to agree with them on first showing. As the US was still not directly involved in the war the tank had no battle record and all the old hands hoped fervently that simply keeping it in running order would be an achievement worth advertising. Colonel Keller had actually issued a special order of the day in June, commending Corporal Ribbins and Troopers Woodgate, Parfitt, Rawlins, Kernahan and Ridpath for the 'courage, determination and devotion' they had shown in maintaining their tanks, often under air attack, while in Greece. Those very soldiers would have exchanged their citation for a reliable fighting vehicle any day.

Compared with contemporary British cruisers, the Honey was marginally better protected but it packed no better punch. Its 37mm gun fired an armour-piercing shell that weighed virtually the same as that fired by the 40mm main armament of the A-9, A-10, A-13, A-15 and Matilda.

There was no high-explosive shell for the 37mm, so as far as its fighting capacity was concerned the Honey suffered from the same handicap as its British-built counterparts. The truth was that the two-pounder and the 37mm were obsolescent by the end of 1941, though both could hit hard given favourable circumstances. Often derided later, the 40mm, with which we had trained so earnestly at Lulworth, put up a good performance in 1940 and drilled holes in the 30mm armour of the Mark III panzers at a respectable range; some claimed to have achieved a knock-out at 1,000 yards, though others doubted this. It had been highly effective against the Italian M11/39, which, even if treated as a joke by us, nevertheless had 30mm armour plate in places, and it could see off the M13/40, which had an even thicker skin and a bigger gun. In the spring of 1941 someone in high places thought enough of the M13/40 to send one of our own armoured regiments into action with machines captured at Beda Fomm the previous winter. This stopgap experiment was not repeated.

Though the two-pounder had been adequate at the beginning of the war, its performance against improved enemy tanks was soon found wanting. By the middle of 1941 the Germans were producing face-hardened steel – rather like putting a glaze on earthenware – which helped to break up solid shot. They were thickening their plate and increasing the size of their guns. Their turrets could take bigger weapons without much trouble; ours were adaptable only with great difficulty. The Matilda, the heavily armoured, slow infantry-support tank, could not be up-gunned at all.

We made the best of what we'd got, simply because we had no choice, and practised hard with the 37mm at a dusty battle camp on the desert side of the Cairo–Fayoum road, where we used knocked-out panzers as targets.

While we trained we tried to make sense of the overall picture in Africa, which had changed dramatically since we had handed over our new cruisers to 2RTR at Mersa Matruh. On 14 February, the day after the British 1st Armoured Brigade was formed for the Greek expedition, with 3RTR and the 4th Hussars as its main tank element, the first vehicles of the Afrika Corps were being swung ashore at Tripoli. The German build-up continued in March and a couple of days after Hitler attacked Yugoslavia and Greece, the Western Desert Force, conquerors of Graziani, terror of the Italians, was bundled out of Libya. General Erwin Rommel, who up to then had been simply a name in the files held by the 'Int' people, became someone to be reckoned with. No one in 3RTR that summer could tell you who had chased us out of Greece but even the sanitary man knew who had captured Red O'Connor and General Neame 'up the blue' near Derna back in April. That was when the siege of Tobruk had begun and it was still besieged when we got our Honeys at the end of August. General Wavell, who had been as famous a name as any known to the troops, had gone from the scene after two attempts to smash the enemy had failed – Operation Brevity in May and Operation Battleaxe in June.

Anyone who had fought in Battleaxe was listened to intently by tank crews. Up until that time the Matilda – more correctly Infantry Tank Mark II – had been considered almost impervious to anti-tank guns. The 4th and 7th RTR had put the wind up the SS Totenkopf Division at Arras in 1940 when their supposedly armour-piercing shells just bounced off the British tanks. It had been the same story with the Italians, and when the Afrika Corps first tangled with the Matildas, its guns also could not get through the armour, up to 78mm thick. War correspondents dubbed the Matilda the 'Queen of the Battlefield'.

During Battleaxe, in the fighting around Solium and Fort Capuzzo, the Queen lost her crown. The Germans had strengthened their positions on and around Halfaya Pass – with reconditioned Italian artillery guns, still lying about after Wavell's early victories, and by digging in batteries of 88mm anti-aircraft guns. They could rely on the Luftwaffe for protection at that time.

Rommel, who had seen the power of the Matildas in France in 1940 when he was commanding the 7th Panzer division, wrote of the 88s '. . . with their barrels horizontal there was practically nothing to be seen above ground. I had great hopes . . . of this arrangement.' His optimism was justified when C Squadron of 4RTR rolled confidently to the attack and was shot to pieces. Only one of its tanks survived the ordeal.

From our side the specific importance of the part played by the 88 was not immediately recognised, as the battlefield and its wrecks were left to the enemy to clean up. The assault had been met with a vast display of firepower, to which the new high-velocity 50mm anti-tank gun, the Pak 38, had also made a contribution. Low slung and easily camouflaged, it fired a four-and-a-half-pound AP shell a long way. And it was the range at which the damage was done that intrigued us. It was disturbing to hear estimates of the range that the enemy was opening fire at being well over 1,000 yards, even 2,000 yards. Our 40mm could send a two-pound shot up to 1,200 yards, but after 500 yards the penetration power dropped sharply and accuracy suffered even more. A gunner would have to be a genius to plant its small AP shot on a dug-in position at more that 1,000 yards. Even then he could not expect to put the crew out of action.

The panzers were another matter, although their reputation grew after Halfaya and Battleaxe. The full extent of the damage they had suffered was obscured because they were able to recover damaged tanks, leaving only a dozen or so wrecks, to be measured against the seventy or so that we had left behind. Nevertheless, even taking into account reports that a version of the Mark III was now armed with a 50mm gun, we felt we would be able to deal with them. At least we knew they could be knocked out by our 40mm guns.

So the training went on and the captured wrecks of panzers received a hammering from our Honeys on range practice. As my gunner, Geordie Reay, put it: 'They're my favourite, Germans, they are. I could spend the rest of the war firing at them.' Geordie was an ex-miner and one of the best tank gunners in the battalion. He was also one of the best cooks.

For two weeks we squadron sergeant majors went off into the desert to study navigation – a field in which I felt we always had the edge on the enemy. The British Army benefited from the experience of years of service in Africa, whereas there aren't many sand dunes in Westphalia and Silesia.

Space was the most awesome thing about the Western Desert. Whatever type of terrain was encountered, there was always plenty of it. The variety was infinite – soft dunes, stony flats, salt marsh, sand with boulders, sand with pebbles, pebbles with pebbles, miles and miles of flat plain, tortuous ravines or wadis, towering limestone escarpments – and hardly a sign that human beings had every passed that way. War relics apart, once the delta had been left behind, there were a few stone cairns, perhaps a ruined mud-walled fort, rare clusters of Bedouin tents, and, even rarer, palms around an oasis.

No one could take liberties with this environment. The dry heat beat down fiercely during the day, while, in winter, the nights were bitterly cold. A good greatcoat was a treasured part of a soldier's kit. The weather in this wilderness was unpredictable. Storms blew up out of nowhere and lasted for an hour or for days. Cloudbursts carpeted the desert with flowers in twenty-four hours and they would wither just as quickly. Dawn could be splendid, with the sun rising majestically to shorten the purple shadows, or it would sneak in miserably through great swatches of mist. A landscape which had been cloaked in fog at daybreak would be dancing in a heat haze by noon so that it was impossible to tell a camel from a burnt-out lorry or a clump of thorns from a Mark IV panzer.

I learned to appreciate the newly delivered American Jeep during our fortnight's navigational instruction using the rather primitive sun compass. The Jeep coped with all obstacles when we travelled deep into the Wadi el Natrun area, previously said to be impassable for tracked and wheeled vehicles alike. On the final run back to base we set out sights on a Coptic monastery just south of Alexandria and at the end of a 'leg' of fifty miles, we were only a few hundred yards from our objective. After a comfortable night as guests of the monks, we gave them a box of surplus rations, to which I added a bottle of whisky. After the kindness their brethren had shown me in Greece I felt I owed it to them.

Beni Yusef camp wasn't the place you would choose for a summer holiday, though it lay within sight of the Pyramids. We shared it with the other regiments of the 4th Armoured Brigade, the 8th Hussars and 5RTR, which made a total of around 160 Honeys to raise the dust. Fortunately, neither Cairo nor Alexandria were too far away, and, though Alexandria was preferable, we visited both. The poverty and dirt in Cairo were indescribable. It was like an oven during the day and was plagued by fat grey flies from the rubbish dumps used by the general public as latrines. Refuse was thrown everywhere and there was no main drainage system as far as I could see. Everywhere there were soldiers drifting about 'chocker-flippin'-block' and browned off, while at the same time glad to get away from the dreariness of the camps. Officers packed the tables under striped umbrellas in the garden of Groppi's cafe, which was famous for its cakes and coffee and its clientele of plump Egyptian beauties. Down at the Gezira Club cricketers put their names on a list if they wanted a game, but you needed to be good. I saw Bob Crisp bowl Wally Hammond there one day in July 1941. There were quite a number of Test players in the Middle East, drawn from South

Africa, Australia and England. The parties in the Snakepit bar under the scoreboard were often better than the game itself.

Cairo was at its best in the cool of the evening, when everyone from peasant to pasha took the air. In aid of a sort of black-out the street lamps had been given a coat of blue paint, but all the bigger houses were brightly lit. The Germans and Italians were unlikely to bomb a place where they had so many spies and where the bulk of the people were as much on their side as ours. It wasn't an Egyptian war; the knowledge that King Farouk would be glad to see the back of our troops encouraged them to sing ribald songs about Queen Farida with even greater gusto.

As a legacy of the British garrisons in Egypt before the war, the wives of quite a few regular officers still had flats in Cairo and Alexandria. I could never make up my mind whether this was a good thing or not. Others moved to Durban where their husbands could still visit them from time to time – panzers permitting.

Speaking personally, I took the opportunity to see all the tourist attractions and accepted invitations to any party that was going. No one knew how long the good times were going to last. We hadn't been given our Honeys for joy-riding. The day would come when we would have to take them over to the other side of the rusty ribbon of barbed wire – about seven feet high and twice as thick – which Marshal Graziani had ordered to be built to mark the border between Mussolini's African empire and Egypt. Beyond it, past the neat little Italian settlements on the coast, which I had admired during our journey to Matruh at the beginning of the year, lay Tobruk and the besieged 70th Division that had taken over from the Australian 9th. Between them and us lay Jerry and the Italians.

We would go looking for them when we were good and ready was the considered opinion at turret level. How, when and where would be arranged by the top brass, of which there seemed to be no shortage – the Staff had become a growth industry.

Wavell, whose name was famous to troops and public alike, had done a straight swap with Sir Claude Auchinlek, Commander-in-Chief, India, of whom few soldiers from Britain had heard. 'The Auk', as the newspapers called him, took over responsibility for the Middle East, including places of no direct interest to us – Iraq, Malta and Palestine.

The old Western Desert Force was relegated to the level of a corps command – one of two being set up. It was numbered XIII, the other being XXX Corps.

To take direct control of the impending battle, a new headquarters was created in September 1941 – Eighth Army. Fresh from his victories over the Italians in East Africa came Lieutenant-General Sir Alan Cunningham to lead it.

Churchill could therefore tell Auchinlek what he wanted, 'The Auk' would pass on the message to Cunningham, who would instruct his corps commanders, who would order the divisions under them to get on with it, and so on. By the time it reached Trooper Jones, the whole thing would come down to two words: 'Driver advance . . .'

The appointments and disappointments of the top brass left 3RTR unmoved. The fact that we were in XXX Corps was of little consequence and I doubt if any of the rank and file knew or cared that Lieutenant-General Sir Willoughby Norrie was in command. Once again, thanks to the BBC, most ordinary soldiers were aware that the 7th Armoured Division was led by 'Strafer' Gott (every tank carried a 'wireless' and reception was excellent). 'Strafer' received a lot of publicity.

Brigadier Alec Gatehouse, who ran the 4th Armoured Brigade, was known to some of the RTR pre-war soldiers because, as a regimental officer, he had taken part in the annual peacetime exercises on Salisbury Plain, but he too was a remote figure to a tank crew. The real interest of gunners, drivers and radio operators lay in the people who most closely affected their chances of survival.

In the long run, of course, this did very much lie in the hands of Gatehouse, Norrie and Cunningham, but as the distances were closing, life and death depended directly on (a) the tank commander, (b) the troop commander, and (c) the squadron leader. Other squadron leaders were someone else's problem. The CO would excite interest according to the extent he could be blamed for getting us into or out of trouble.

Chapter Seven

Operation Crusader

Operation Crusader began for us at last light on 17 November, which was about 6 p.m. At a given moment hundreds of ungainly box-shaped vehicles roared into life, emitting fumes and smoke, and started to lumber across the desert. Some days earlier we had camouflaged our Honeys at a depot well behind the frontier, hiding the turrets under rigid canopies of sackcloth and canvas so that from the air they would look like three-ton lorries.

Having driven about eighty miles to our concentration area, still on the Egyptian side of the frontier, we drew up in the guise of a lorry park. There was a mild panic the morning after this overnight trek, as a number of commanders reported their rubber tracks damaged, probably when crossing a bad stretch of sharp limestone. We waited for spares to arrive from the delta before moving once more, this time to our jumping-off line. There were a number of scares about cracks in the tracks when we first got the Honeys, but they seemed to go on regardless.

On the 13th the colonel had returned from a conference at 'Brigade' and sent for the squadron commanders. George Witheridge (B Squadron commander), a member of the sergeant's mess who had been commissioned after Calais, came back with the 'gen' and said we could be going into action at any time from then on. Having led the squadron in Greece, 'Withers' had a pretty shrewd idea what we were likely to come up against. During the three days that we subsequently remained at the same position, we spent a lot of time checking every tank's equipment and ammunition, under my supervision as squadron sergeant major.

The battle plan – although at troop level the details emerged only later – was simple enough: two left hooks towards the coast, where most of the German tanks were concentrated. The bulk of our infantry and the slow, heavy Matildas and Valentines was placed under General Godwin-Austen's XIII Corps, which was to pin down and crush the garrisons holding Bardia, Solium and Halfaya on the frontier. The fast cruiser tanks were concentrated in XXX Corps under Norrie, with the object of thrusting wider towards Tobruk. Forced to counter this threat, the enemy armour would be destroyed as it attacked us in positions of our own choosing. Once this had been done, '70 Div' would sally forth and the 1st South African Division would join up with them, while the XIII Corps troops advanced along the coast. The siege would be over, the way to Tripoli open. So much for the theory – even in retrospect, it doesn't seem such a bad plan.

There was a general feeling that the troops would give a good account of themselves. The two divisions in XIII Corps had been brought up to strength, 4th Indian after its experiences during Battleaxe, and the New Zealand following its ordeals in Greece and Crete. There were no doubts about their fighting qualities.

It was less easy to predict the performance of XXX Corps under General Norrie, and it may be as well to take a closer look at the formations.

HQ 7th Armoured Division

Experienced and under the desert veteran 'Strafer' Gott.

7th Armoured Brigade:

7th Hussars
2RTR
6RTR

Many of the personnel had fought in the Libyan campaign but the equipment had also seen service. Though half the tanks were A-15 Crusaders, the rest, some seventy or so, were of the older A-13 type and there were even a few vintage A-10s. Despite the repairs that had been carried out, the brigade could expect losses due to breakdowns.

7th Motorised Support Group
Under the leadership of the tough Brigadier Jock Campbell, contained a regiment of twenty-five-pounders and a battalion of the Rifle Brigade.

4th Armoured Brigade
8th Hussars
3RTR
5RTR

There was a large proportion of seasoned troops among the regiments, but the Honeys were still an unknown quantity. With the addition of an artillery regiment (twenty-five-pounders) and the 2nd Scots Guards in lorries, we formed a powerful 'brigade group'.

22nd Armoured Brigade
3rd County of London Yeomanry
4th County of London Yeomanry
2nd Royal Gloucestershire Hussars

None of these regiments had been in action before. Each was equipped with over fifty new Crusaders, which had spent some time in workshops to be modified for desert conditions. The 22nd Brigade was not as strong as the 4th in either artillery or infantry.

2nd South African Division
Contained the 1st, 4th and 5th infantry brigades which had seen action briefly in East Africa and looked fit and hard.

A violent thunderstorm broke as we bedded down in the early hours of the 18th. Many crews unshipped their canopies and used them to shelter from the lashing rain. At daybreak, with camouflage replaced, we resumed our march in and, observing strict radio silence, crossed a desert from which all previous tracks had been washed. The airflow caused by our speed came cold from the damp earth. We passed without incident through the gaps blown in Graziani's border wire and queued at fuel dumps like motorists on a garage forecourt on a bank holiday. The Honey's need to be filled up every forty miles or so was a serious weakness; with 160 tanks in our brigade alone, vast quantities of high-octane aviation spirit were required, so it was reassuring to find it waiting for us.

The rain had laid the dust and we rolled on deep into enemy territory without raising the usual clouds. Not a single hostile aircraft appeared. Mile after mile went by and by mid-afternoon, after refuelling again and shedding camouflage, the brigade was advancing in battle formation: the Honeys in line abreast 100 yards apart, 200 yards between waves. It was a stirring sight, the sand-coloured paintwork barely scratched, each turret bearing its squadron marking – a triangle for A, square for B, circle for C and diamond for HQ – all in 3RTR green like our shoulder flash. Above us fluttered little yellow pennants, picturesque but dangerous. It hadn't taken the enemy long to work out that the more pennants there were on a wireless antenna, the more important the target. No one was sorry when they disappeared later in the war, but on 18 November they were considered to be an essential guide to recognition – the Germans and Italians didn't fly them. Certainly the pennants added a touch of dash to the scene as did the armoured cars of the 1st King's Dragoon Guards racing far ahead. Somewhere to our left, because we were on the inner flank of the strike force, the 7th Brigade, and beyond them the 22nd, were advancing in similar fashion – some 480 tanks in all, give or take the inevitable breakdowns.

Formidable was the only description for this thundering herd. A group of enemy recce vehicles obviously thought so and, just as the light began to fail, burst from cover and fled, pursued by flurries of tracer bullets. They probably fired back but no casualties were reported. Night fell and calm was restored. The squadrons rallied, formed column and drove a short distance to leaguer positions. Four-gallon 'flimsies', which leaked all over the lorries carrying them, were used to refuel the Honeys yet again.

That first night things were done according to the book. I posted the guards on the leaguer, got my orders from Withers as to the time of reveille, checked the ammunition state (not difficult as hardly any had been fired), confirmed the wireless net had closed down and, having enjoyed a meal cooked by the crew of my own tank, finally joined them under the tarpaulin stretched from the side of the Honey. If the events of the day had made a painful impression anywhere, it was on my bottom. The man who designed the Honey had forgotten to provide the commander with a seat. Our fitters had welded hooks inside the turret from which a strip of canvas could be slung but it proved to be a most uncomfortable perch.

Break of day, 19 November. The tight leaguers broke up and the battalion's tanks took up positions 100 yards apart and 'stood to'. A swift brew up and a cold breakfast, and we were off, having received the radio codes for the day and sundry map references. From that moment until the end of December maps were to dominate my every waking hour. Day after day I toiled to discover where we had been, where we were and where we were hoping to go. As squadron sergeant major, my job was to navigate the squadron throughout the operation. Withers had touching faith in my navigational prowess and from time to time this encouraged the CO to ask for confirmation or reassurance. It was not a subject on which bluff, a soldier's best friend, was any good at all. Guesswork got men killed.

The Crusader operation included readily identifiable features, in particular the escarpments which step down to the Mediterranean, but there were also large inscrutable flat areas. Names marked on the map boldly as Gabr Saleh or Bir Berraneb are simply figments of a cartographer's imagination. Show me signs of civilisation at Tmimi or the now infamous Gazala. Look around and you may find a well in a shady hollow, but little more.

Swaying in my numbing sling seat in the cupola of the Honey, I clutched my talc-covered map and studied it with religious fervour as the squadron raced over the plain on the heels of the Kings Dragoon Guards, whose Daimlers were in hot pursuit of their Afrika Corps counterparts.

If there were any landmarks I made a note of them. Each small track we crossed was recorded. When we halted I took compass readings if possible, checked the sun with the time and the time with the sun. Shadow lengths became an obsession. Direction had played little part in my previous combat experience as it had nearly always taken me in the same direction, towards the rear, in the company of any number of people who knew not only 'the way', but 'the quickest way'. During Crusader I was acutely aware that if you got it wrong going forward you were likely to be redirected by a signpost made in Germany. There were any number of natural hazards lurking. It was not considered good form to remind a certain Hussar regiment that it had left a complete squadron's worth of undamaged light tanks in an unsuspected sea of soft sand.

From a number of articles and books on the war in the desert it is possible to get the idea that bringing the enemy to battle was the easiest part of the exercise. Far from it. The commanders might lay down the centre line ('Charlie Love') for an operation but after that it was up to the navigators to make the best of the gyrations which followed, not all of which appeared logical or desirable.

It occurred to me as we pounded after our quarry that if the German recce troops were behaving as ours would have done in similar circum-stances, they would not be indulging in aimless flight, but would be drawing us towards some cold-eyed colleagues less inclined to concede right of passage.

This, of course, was what our elders and betters were hoping for. They wanted to bring on a clash in which our more numerous forces destroyed the Axis armour and were concerned lest the enemy declined to play the game. Some hope. Yet, according to subsequent well-researched accounts, Cunningham managed to achieve such a complete surprise that Rommel was under the impression that the British elements first reported were simply a reconnaissance force similar to one his own troops had carried out a short time previously.

Certainly, the stray enemy vehicles we saw fled in panic and Bob Crisp, who was a way ahead of the rest of the battalion with C Squadron, reported having attacked and dispersed an enemy column, destroying two or three light tanks, and then driving on until he came in sight of the light-house at Bardia and the sea.

During this sortie he came on the air to the CO and made some rude remarks about the time it was taking the other squadrons to catch up, in particular ours, which was tasked with keeping in touch with 5RTR on our left. Certainly I never saw the sea. We fired on a small group of enemy tanks but in the afternoon I found myself plotting a course to the west to take us back to the rest of the brigade. A battle group of some 100 tanks had come booming out of the sun and attacked the 8th Hussars. This brought 5RTR dashing ten miles to their aid and we were also expected to join in. By the time we reached the area darkness had fallen.

In leaguer that night we learned that the Hussars had lost twenty tanks, though some were only damaged. The 5th had lost three. Both units claimed to have knocked out several panzers.

A severe action had also been fought by the 22nd Armoured Brigade. They had clashed with the Ariete at Bir-el-Gubi and – with Crusaders breaking down and the Italian tanks and guns firing from their well-prepared and concealed positions – had lost about half their strength.

It had been a very severe first action for the 4th County of London Yeomanry and the 2nd Gloucestershire Hussars.

The good news was that the 7th Armoured Brigade, without appreciable opposition, had got through to the airfield at Sidi Rezegh and surprised the enemy while planes were still in the process of taking off. Ten miles from the perimeter of the Tobruk defences, it looked to be an ideal area for concentrating a relieving force. According to the map it was overlooked by an escarpment and set on a plain which ended in another escarpment.

We leaguered a few miles from the rest of the 4th Armoured Brigade that night, some of our scattered troops arriving well into the night. Lorries came up and off-loaded flimsies under my supervision so that the squadron could start with full fuel tanks in the morning. Not a lot of damage or mechanical trouble was reported and we began to appreciate the better points of the Honey. One question that crossed my mind was the reasoning behind the brigade groupings. Why had the three inexperienced yeomanry regiments been put in the same formation, albeit with the most experienced armoured car regiment, the 11th Hussars? Why had they been given the most modern Crusaders, when the 7th Armoured – desert experts – had second-hand tanks? It was beyond me. No doubt it would make sense to someone. In any case, the 7th had reached Sidi Rezegh, despite their A-13s.

Chapter Eight

Sidi Rezegh: What a Shambles!

One desert airfield was apt to look very much like another. Someone would select a likely place, iron out any bumps, erect a windsock and a few tents and, with the arrival of fuel tankers and a couple of wireless lorries, they were in business. There were quite a few in the Libyan 'Big Bulge' and Sidi Rezegh was no real exception. It only seemed worse because of our obsession with it that winter.

It was probably chosen originally because it was near the Trigh el Abd, the broad beaten track which ran from the frontier and passed south of Tobruk. About five miles from it there was a white marabout, or tomb, which must have been very helpful to pilots.

I can only assume that Sidi Rezegh, whoever he was, didn't like company. Only a hermit would have wanted to live on that oven-shelf of plateau which must have been a forbidding place at the best of times, and when I first set eyes on it, it was definitely not at its best. The ferocious battle raging for its possession had turned it into a giant ashtray full of glowing embers and smouldering stubs. It had taken us two bewildering days to get there.

Someone later described Crusader as the 'whirlwind battle', but whirlpool would have been nearer the mark as we all went round in ever decreasing circles until we were sucked onto the rocks at Sidi Rezegh.

The days were short – about twelve hours of fighting light from 6 a.m. After dark a large proportion of the units on both sides trekked out into the desert to a quiet spot to refuel, rearm, repair and eat while the commanders worked out the conundrums for the next day.

For about forty-eight hours 3RTR pursued or were pursued by one section or other of the Afrika Corps. On the afternoon of the 20th a furious battle flared up, during which we were driven back somewhere around our starting point at Gabr Saleh and were reinforced by 5RTR. Finally, the whole of 22nd Armoured Brigade was ordered to support the 4th and must have exerted pressure somewhere because by dusk the enemy opposing us faded away. Quite a few Honeys had been knocked out and the total losses of the brigade, including those lost by the Hussars the previous day, reduced it to around 100 tanks. Many hits were claimed on panzers but as we were falling back most of the time there was little evidence of knock-outs.

A couple of hours' sleep, huddled in a turret or under a tarpaulin that didn't quite keep out the driving rain, and we were off again, this time in pursuit of a battle group which drew steadily away across a sea of steaming mud.

The framework of the battalion had begun to change at this stage and squadron leaders were forming their remaining tanks into improvised troops of differing numbers, according to the experience of the surviving commanders. There had been a number of casualties. Captain Peter Williams, who had won the Military Cross when Bill Reeves broke out from Calais, was among the dead, as were two of my friends, Sergeants Blackshaw and Knight.

Progress was slow. There was nothing very clever about the enemy tactics, which were simply common sense. They had recently introduced the towed 50mm anti-tank gun, the Pak 38, which could penetrate 50mm of armour at 1,000 yards. Although the piece was long it was mounted on a low carriage and easily concealed.

The Mark IIIs and IVs, some of which had extra plates bolted on their existing armour, could engage us at extreme range. As we tried to close, under fire from their turret guns, which were at least as good as ours, they could pick a moment to fall back and let the Pak 38s come into action. The Paks, having laid down their four-and-a-half-pound shot, could withdraw in their turn, covered by a few 88s, 3,000 yards from us, while the tanks took up new positions. When the 88s withdrew the whole cycle began all over again. Artillery observers travelled with battalion headquarters but in the ebb and flow of the battle they had a difficult task directing our twenty-five-pounders. Better spotting from the air was the real answer and for once the RAF was on top of the situation. Unhappily, practical liaison systems didn't exist. The Honeys were forced to rely on their own guns and their greater speed – though this carried a penalty as it burned more fuel.

Various tactics were tried to overcome the problem. Bob Crisp, for all his cavalier approach to life, had a very logical streak and put into practice a drill he devised on the ranges at battle camp. Under the training methods applicable at the time, if a hull-down position was not practical, commanders were expected to engage while on the move. Bob, who as a fast bowler had a wonderful eye, would not accept this. His system is best described in his own words:

> . . . after the target had been indicated . . . a more or less automatic procedure followed if the circumstances were favourable. The objective was to get close enough to the enemy tank to be able to destroy it. The first order, then, was 'Driver advance flat out'. The gunner would do his best to keep the cross-wires of his telescopic sight on the target all the time we were moving. The next order, heard by the gunner, driver and loader would be 'Driver halt'. As soon as the tank stopped and he was on target, the gunner would fire without further command . . . The sound of the shot was the signal for the driver to let in his clutch and be off again.

With practice the tank would be stationary for only four seconds. This procedure was adopted by most tank commanders and proved effective. As all the German tanks were slower than Crusaders and Honeys, the sprint–stop–shoot tactics were appropriate for the open desert but they did nothing to solve the problem of the defensive screen of Pak 38s and their bigger brethren.

It was not until mid-afternoon that we drew within striking distance of Sidi Rezegh, which was hidden by a low mushroom cloud from the base of which came thumps, booms, rumblings and streaks of lightning. Gradually we arrived at the top of the escarpment and looked down on a scene which bewildered as much as it shocked. As far as one could see, until vision was defeated by a swirling haze, there were motionless wrecks some hundreds of yards apart, others in groups, facing in all directions. Some were black and silent, others smouldering and crackling, and a few were blazing brightly, black smoke curling busily up into the dirty sky. Geysers of dirt shot up haphazardly among this flotsam.

Up to this point I had been able to give Trooper Trotter, my stolid Yorkshire gunner who had taken over from Geordie Reay, control of the 37mm, but now this was clearly impossible. Something unpleasant was happening on the far edge of the airfield, where dust clouds indicated an attack in progress, though who was attacking could only be guessed. Not only was the plain littered with knocked-out tanks, lorries, armoured cars and gun-towing quads, but there were weapon pits, silent twenty-five-pounders, upturned Bren carriers, staff cars and, here and there – regardless of the shellburst – men digging or walking about as if they had not noticed what was going on about them. From a distant ridge, yellow flashes reminded me of the batteries firing from the hills at Calais.

I don't know how long we paused on the brink of this scene of utter confusion but obviously it was as long as it took the brigadier to make up his mind whether or not to commit us. My operator, Lance Corporal Gibson, who could guess what was going on from the wireless traffic without being able to see anything himself, was looking up at me with a shocked expression but said nothing. Trotter, who never wasted words, remained staring through the rubber eye-piece of the sight. God knows what went through the mind of my driver, Lance Corporal Colclough, who could see only a patch of dirty daylight on the ridge through his observation slit. I warned him on the intercom that if we went 'down there' he would have to look out for our own infantry who were still around.

For the loader: 'Make sure you've plenty of ammunition for the 37 at hand.' I didn't think it would be safe to use the Browning.

For the gunner: 'We'll have to be sure before we fire, Trot. A group of Honeys has been sent to recce that lot.'

The buzzing and crackling in the headphone I was holding to one ear cleared.

'Orders . . .'

The CO was telling Withers that we were going in with 5RTR on our right; the 22nd Armoured Brigade was also attacking – with the enemy believed to be the 21st Panzer Division.

'Advance now . . .'

The Honey jerked and dipped, and we went plunging down a stony gully – like one of the chines at Bournemouth, only covered with camel scrub. Seen from afar the panorama had been like a Hollywood spectacular. At close quarters the airfield was nothing more than a sordid cemetery covered with open graves and funeral pyres. Dead gunners and infantry sprawled everywhere beside smashed weapons. Ahead, red glows and dark smudges indicated the oncoming enemy but shells were arriving from all sides. Having given Trotter a likely target – a big black blob – I shrank to eye level in the turret as splinters cracked and clunked on the sides of the Honey. Dust and tiny fragments flew about the fighting compartment.

'Left stick – left a bit more – now right . . .'

We jerked through a group of wrecks but, before I could confirm the target I had selected, a Honey raced out of a wall of smoke and crossed our line of fire. It was followed immediately by two more. Yet another weaved slowly after them, tattered bedrolls flapping behind the turret.

'Beer – Beer One – what the hell is happening? Over.'

'I—I think the yo-yo boys are having a crack at us. And friends on our right are being attacked by anti-tank guns . . .'

A shattering roar and a pillar of flame announced a direct hit close at hand. The enemy gunners were pounding 5RTR, who, trying to get round the flank, were edging left into the path of our advance. Soon Honeys were careering all over the place and only the quick reactions of the driver saved us from a collision. From a distance the battered yeomanry regiments of 22nd Armoured Brigade concluded that only Mark IIIs would indulge in such a display of fury and added 40mm shot to the missiles screaming around us. Both RTR battalions became inextricably mixed. As each was on a different radio frequency there was no simple way of restoring order and messages were passed urgently by the two colonels through the rear link tanks to the brigadier, who then sent back his orders by the same route. We were to withdraw to the south-west.

*   *   *

An even wilder rodeo followed as tanks reversed, swung around, narrowly missed each other or, in some cases, didn't. The sight of this was too much for the enemy who halted and began to withdraw – baffled, perhaps, and clearly short of ammunition and fuel.

Not many who had started out so confidently on 17 November were still with the regiment. Squadrons and troops had been reformed so often that they bore little resemblance to the originals.

Bob Crisp had been severely wounded in the head; I had been alongside his tank when it was hit and evacuated him and another member of his tank crew on the back of my tank. Although other units in the brigade, 8th Hussars and 5RTR, were returned to the delta for refitting, 3RTR remained with 7th Support Group, sustaining further casualties in a tank battle near Antelat, losing six tanks. We were eventually ordered back to Egypt on 26 December after some twenty-eight days of continuous operations.

Chapter Nine

Back to the Delta

Sidi Rezegh was a severe battle for 3RTR and casualties were heavy. The cream of the battalion went west and it was never quite the same. For me, the operation confirmed my conviction that it 'did not pay to make special pals'. Too many friendships were cut short.

The men who survived the drawn-out struggle returned to Egypt, not having slept under a roof for more than two months. For most of the time the weather had been cold and wet, making life even more miserable. Those who came back from Crusader and Sidi Rezegh were all lean and weather-beaten and, though we craved fresh meat and vegetables, we considered we had never been fitter. We were tired but encouraged by the thought of a fairly long spell in the flesh-pots of Cairo and Alexandria.

I was afflicted with desert sores. Everywhere you moved in a tank you caught yourself on metal; if you got dirt, sand or oil in the cuts, they virtually never healed while you were out in the desert. Once we got back to the delta they cleared up as if by magic. I was also prone to severe sunburn and during spells in the desert my face 'skinned' every three or four days.

From January to March 1942 we enjoyed our time in Cairo whilst refitting the tanks and receiving replacement tank crews; our casualties at lower levels had been heavy. Officer casualties had also been severe: our CO, Lieutenant Colonel Bunny Ewins, had left due to illness, two squadron commanders had been badly wounded and most troop commanders were casualties – replacements had to be found.

Our new CO was most welcome – Lieutenant Colonel 'Pip' Roberts, an RTR officer who I had known as a subaltern in 3RTR before the war. He had served as brigade major in 4th Armoured Brigade during General O'Connor's successful campaign and was highly regarded as a tank tactician. Two new squadron commanders, Major Jim Hutton and Major

Alec Doig also joined us at the same time and were most successful in helping to weld the battalion back into a formidable fighting force.

We also received several replacement troop officers, though more were required. I and another sergeant, Bud Harned, who had won the DCM during Operation Crusader, were recommended for immediate commissions by the squadron commanders. We were interviewed by our new CO, seen by the divisional commander, Major General Jock Campbell, VC, and approved.

It was normal on being commissioned from the ranks to be sent to an Officer Cadet Training Unit (OCTU) for six months but this would have meant returning to the UK and Sandhurst. Colonel Roberts, in urgent need of troop commanders, vetoed this idea, the paperwork was completed on the spot and we merely went from the sergeants' mess into the officers' mess.

I drew my special kit allowance of £48, had two days' leave in Cairo, got myself re-kitted and reported back to my new squadron commander, Major Jim Hutton, sporting two shiny new pips on each shoulder. As I had been commissioned from the rank of warrant officer, second class (WO II), I automatically became the senior subaltern in the battalion with the rank of full lieutenant. I was appointed troop commander of No 3 Troop in A Squadron, Recce Squadron.

During my short hectic leave in Cairo I had taken the opportunity to visit one or two places of entertainment, places which had previously been out of bounds to other ranks, such as Shepherds Hotel, Groppi's and Madame Bardia's. Madame Bardia's was very up-market and it was possible to meet most of General HQ (GHQ), staff officers and even King Farouk on occasions.

Whilst at Madame Bardia's on my first evening, I made the acquaintance of Assizza, one of her famous belly dancers. We became quite friendly and on subsequent leaves in Cairo we met quite often. I would be greeted with, 'Ah, Beel! You come back.' It was shortly after I had spent an evening with Assizza in her sumptuous apartments that I was told she was King Farouk's favourite dancer and I was warned it would be wise to discontinue visits. I took the hint.

A Squadron was equipped with the American General Stuart tank, fast and light, but only fitted with a 37mm gun. As the heavy squadrons, A and B were also being equipped with the American General Grant tank, newly arrived in the delta. This was to be the first tank we had that was fitted with a 75mm gun and capable of firing both HE and AP shot, most welcome news to the tank crews. Up until now we had only enjoyed the dubious pleasure of tanks fitted with a two–pounder gun firing AP shot.

In addition, the Grant was also fitted with a 37mm gun in the turret, making it the best armoured tank to date. It was fairly fast with a possible road speed of about 25mph, well armoured, and considered to be capable of outshooting an enemy tank or anti-tank gun, with the exception of the 88mm. The Grant crews found their new tank and armourment ideal and we looked forward to meeting the panzers more or less on even terms.

I was in the process of finding my feet as an officer and breaking in my troop. Many of my replacement crews had come from other units – 8th Hussars, 4th Hussars and other cavalry regiments – but they were all tank trained and very soon fitted in with us tankies. I was ably assisted in this work by my two corporal tank commanders, Kite and Reay, who by this time were considered to be veterans.

Following a last exercise deep in the Wadi Natrun area we were at last considered to be ready for our next trip 'up the blue'. We were now part of the 4th Armoured Brigade, the original 'Desert Rats', our sister units being the 8th Hussars and 5RTR.

We moved up to our positions in the line, part of the way by rail, the remainder on our tracks. The Eighth Army had settled down once more to improve its defences, train and prepare for another attack. It occupied a line west of Tobruk that ran for forty-five miles from Gazala on the coast to Bir Hacheim, a desolate watering hole around which defensive positions had been blasted, mainly from solid rock. Our infantry units held a series of self-contained positions along the front, protected by minefields; these were called 'boxes'. The 4th Armoured Brigade were positioned in the rear of these so-called boxes and we had been told that it was possible Rommel might launch his attack on or about 28 May.

We stayed in this location for several weeks, practising our moves to battle positions should Rommel decide to attempt a right-hook swing south of Bir Hacheim. It was a most trying time in most uncomfortable circumstances. Temperatures at midday were in excess of 110 degrees and life in the tank was almost unbearable; even the flies dropped dead inside. It was also possible to fry an egg on the back of the tank. To make matters worse, it was the season of the khamseen, the hot wind which comes up from the southern Sahara, blows up in a matter of moments and can last for two or three days. It is impossible to do anything whilst these winds are blowing and certainly no movement was possible, visibility being down to about ten yards at best. One good point was that they affected the enemy in exactly the same way.

During this waiting time we practised moving to our battle positions several times. Therefore it was not surprising when the alarm was sounded that Rommel was really on the move, that most of us thought that this was just another practice round.

We were very soon to learn that this time it was for real.

Chapter Ten

The Gazala Battle

The Afrika Corps going about its business was never a pretty sight. Seen through binoculars at 3,000 yards range it looked positively evil, even on a fine spring morning.

The uneasiness that had afflicted the leaguer all night had been well founded. Most people had been busy about the place in the half darkness from about 3.30 a.m. An unusual number of flares had been drifting down in the direction of the 3rd Indian Motor Brigade, which was occupying a ridge about nine miles away on the extreme left flank of the Gazala position.

We knew the location well as it had been reconnoitred and chosen as one of a number of potential battle positions. All Brigade HQ had to do was give the code word and we would be off.

We 'stood to' without incident until about 6 a.m. and managed to get a decent breakfast; then at 7.30 a.m. the code word came. 'Mount – start-up,' and the battalion, which by this time was packed and ready, was on its way, A Squadron leading, my troop on the right.

The Honeys covered about two miles at speed, then halted to take a closer look at the dust and the persistent but obscure movement ahead. As the whole of the 4th Armoured Brigade had been ordered to rendezvous at a given map reference before moving up to the ridge, the cloud could have been raised by 'friends', though 3RTR was supposed to be at the head of a wedge formation with the 8th Hussars on the left and 5RTR on the right.

The mysterious shadows in the murk didn't look friendly. Before we could positively identify them the colonel came on the radio–telephone (RT) and told Jim Hutton, my OC, that the Indians had been overrun during the night – better look out.

We didn't have far to look. The haze which was already hindering observation could not hide the fact that only a panzer group moved in such a deliberate fashion, extended over a broad front, speed carefully regulated to aid command and control and to save fuel.

We drove forward to take a closer look. From 2,000 yards, the swimming images solidified and became Mark IIIs and Mark IVs, row upon row of them. The column stretched into the impenetrable distance. The kernel of Jim Hutton's report was in the phrase, '. . . I say again, 200 tanks.' If this was an exaggeration, it was not outrageous. I started counting them carefully – one, two, three, four – up to twenty in the front rank and they were coming on faster than I at first thought. The range was closing to 1,500 yards. The rest of the battalion were 2,000 yards behind us.

Now for the number of lines of tanks – one, two, three, four ...

'OK, Dodo [the B Squadron call sign] – move to your right **NOW**. We're taking up battle position on the ridge immediately in your rear figures one five zero zero yards – detach figures one troop to take up position on the left flank where we expect friends shortly. A Squadron to protect our left flank. Off to you.'

The CO went on to give orders to the Grant squadrons and we hurried out of the line of fire.

Flashes came from the panzers and loud cracks overhead told of the passage of shells.

B and C squadrons formed a long line, obtaining as much shelter from the ridge as the low 75mm sponson would allow. At about 1,200 yards the CO gave the same order to open fire and in naval terms the action became general.

The 15th Panzer Division (as they were later identified) must have experienced a severe shock. They were using their normal tactics with anti-tank guns, up to 88mm calibre, deployed behind the advancing waves. Believing they were facing tanks armed only with two-pounders – they may even have assumed after seeing the Recce Squadron that the Grants were Honeys – they slowed at a distance, which under normal circumstances would have required us to close with them and suffer the inevitable consequences. Instead they met concentrated and destructive fire.

79

The Grant's 75mm M-2 sponson gun fired a fourteen-pound shell which could cause severe damage at 1,500 yards and penetrate the thickest armour of a Mark III at 1,200 yards.

Furthermore the Grants had the additional fire power of their 37mm turrets, equal in this case to two squadrons of Honeys or Crusaders. As flame spurted from the line of tanks, a positive blizzard of high-grade steel whipped over the level ground.

Hits were scored by both sides almost immediately. Panzers that had been inching forward slewed to a halt as bits flew off them. A couple of Grants caught fire. One tank blew up. Through the spreading smoke crews could be seen stumbling to the rear.

Ever since the first AP shot whistled past me at Calais, I had worn my earphones round my neck in the belief that I could better judge the direction from which shells were coming. In the opening exchange on that featureless ridge near Bir Hacheim the sounds merged for a moment to form an excruciating 'battle static'. Concerned to look out for 5RTR coming up on our flank I swept the ground with my glasses and gave Trotter, my gunner, control of the 37mm. A glance into the turret showed feverish activity as the loader jerked the lever to let the empty case fall and rammed in another. Every few minutes I ordered, 'Driver, advance right a few yards' or 'Driver, reverse left'. The Grants were big enough to stand and slug it out but a Honey had to make it as difficult as possible for the opposing gunners.

During a brief pause to stack more ammunition ready at hand, my loader, Trooper Allwood, attracted my attention and pointed to the head-phones. I listened in and gathered from the brief snatches of conversation that the 8th Hussars had been taken by surprise and forced to come into action around the leaguer area before they could deploy properly. After suffering severe casualties in a brave fight at close range they had been reduced to single figures. The pall of smoke to the far left probably marked the site of the disaster.

In 3RTR the Grants continued to engage the enemy, but as fast as one Panzer was knocked out in the front rank, another crawled up from the rear to take its place. It was clear this could not go on indefinitely. Already the tempo of the gunfire was beginning to fall, even though our own artillery men, the Chestnut Troop of the 1st Royal Horse Artillery (RHA), had been quick to join in and were plastering distant targets. As more and more German anti-tank guns came into action on the ground, the Grants began to suffer. Proof against most panzer guns, their armour could not keep out the 75s and 88s. I could see one or two of our machines reversing slowly out of action with guns cocked up at ridiculous angles. Others, stranded with severed tracks, kept up spasmodic fire from one or other of their guns. Bigger guns meant bigger rounds but not so many of them. Two guns meant two gunners, two loaders. With six in the crew, there was not so much room for ammunition.

B and C squadrons had halted along a low ridge and were engaging the enemy panzers with great effect. The advancing panzers were literally stopped in their tracks, some swerving to a halt with fragments flying from them, some bursting into flames with crewmen leaping to safety.

I had been told to move out to the right flank and to keep an eye out for 5RTR, who were coming to our support. My gunner and loader didn't need any advice or orders from me; they were busily engaged in taking on the enemy panzers, which were still advancing, albeit slowly. Although the Grants were giving a good account of themselves, they were receiving casualties and I could see several burning furiously. We were being hit by all sorts of things and it was difficult to see what was going on. The air stank from the thick cordite fumes and our eyes were red-rimmed and streaming. Now and then there would be a terrific thud and the inside filled with dust and sparks as the tank rocked on its bogies.

Despite the noise and the smoke, however, we were still scoring hits. Lance Corporal Trotter, my gunner, ecstatically informed me he had scored direct hits on two panzers at almost point-blank range and seen their crews bail out.

I had become a little isolated from the rest of my squadron but had been receiving instructions 'on the air' from Jim Hutton to try and maintain contact with 5RTR.

We were using ammunition at a tremendous rate and I was somewhat relieved when the CO came on the air and ordered us to reverse slowly while continuing to engage. Whilst doing so I came upon a knocked-out Grant with the crew standing miserably beside it. It was Bud Harned's tank; his head had been taken clean off by a shell at the beginning of the action.

Shortly after, I felt a tremendous crash on my tank followed by a yell from below to bail out: we had become a broadside target for a number of enemy panzers that had crept closer, almost unseen in the murk and dust. An armour-piercing shot had penetrated the front plate, slightly wounding Lance Corporal Colclough, the driver. When I checked the tank after bailing out I was surprised to find we had been hit five times without being penetrated.

I took over the fourth tank in my troop, the corporal tank commander somewhat dismayed at being told to dismount. I retained Trotter and Allwood who were unharmed, but took over the spare driver, Trooper Evans. Lance Corporal Colclough was not severely wounded but needed treatment; he returned to duty some three or four weeks later.

By now most of the Grants were out of action; the remainder were being rallied by Colonel Pip Roberts and were still engaging the advancing panzers. Colonel Pip himself, with about seven Grants, was now heavily engaged by enemy tanks and one or two 88mm anti-tank guns which had come up to support the panzers.

A Squadron, or what was left of it, was to try and outflank the enemy but the situation was so involved and communication so bad that we remained out on the right flank, still hoping that 5RTR would come to our rescue.

At this point Colonel Pip's tank was hit and disabled, the shell passing through the nose of the tank and out at the back, but all of the crew were unharmed. It did mean that the CO had to change tanks, which took a bit of time at such a critical stage of the battle.

The next few days seemed to consist of a series of orders, counter-orders and, at times, complete disorder. 3RTR, very much depleted, first moved north-east, attached to 22nd Armoured Brigade, then next day south-east of Bir Harmet. The battalion was now down to seven Grants and twelve Honeys. With my squadron commander, Jim Hutton, badly wounded and evacuated, and the loss of two troop commanders – one killed and the other, Alec Doig, wounded – our officer strength was depleted. To make matters worse, George Witheridge, the one remaining squadron commander, was also hit, receiving shell splinters in the eyes, and he too had to go back.

We were then told to return to the 4th Armoured Brigade area and here we picked up a few more of the battalion tanks that had somehow become isolated. We now had a battalion strength of fifteen Grants and fourteen Honeys, including Colonel Pip's Grant and two Regimental HQ (RHQ) Honeys. There was only myself with 3 Troop and Johnny Dunlop with 4 Troop left as troop commanders.

We now received orders from the CO – directly, in the absence of Jim Hutton – to proceed with all speed to an escarpment some two miles ahead. Unfortunately, around this time a sandstorm had sprung up and visibility was down to about ten yards. The only thing to do was halt and try to hold the tanks together and hope that visibility would improve. Sure enough, the weather did improve and we set off again for the escarpment, with Johnny Dunlop's troop on my left. We were 2,000 yards in front of the Grants and battalion HQ, and were to halt when we reached the escarpment and await further orders.

When we reached the escarpment we found there were only two tracks leading to the top. I reported this back to the CO and received more orders to push on up to the top and take up positions of protection whilst the heavy tanks made their ascent up the very steep tracks.

On reaching the top we immediately came under fire from enemy tanks, which were holding excellent positions 1,000 yards to the west. Again, my tank was hit, forcing me to bail out, with the driver and gun loader/operator being slightly wounded. I could see that two of Dunlop's tanks had also been hit, but with our backs to the escarpment it was difficult to find a safe spot. The Grants had now made their way up the escarpment and with a battery of twenty-five-pounders in support, engaged the enemy at close range, inflicting a number of casualties in a matter of moments. The gallant gunners were firing over open sights at ranges of 600 to 800 yards and were most effective.

The Grants were now under the command of Captain Granton, an officer who had only recently joined us, and, although they were giving a good account of themselves, they were receiving casualties. We had only been in action about fifteen minutes but already the Grants were down to six tanks and the Honeys to five. I had now transferred to another of my troop tanks and had only one other tank beside me.

We were then dealt a crushing blow when Colonel Pip's tank was hit and burst into flames. The CO and his adjutant, who travelled in the same tank, were both badly burnt, the 75mm gunner was killed, the wireless operator was seriously wounded and the 37mm gunner was also badly burnt. We managed to get the wounded down the escarpment to where Doctor MacMillan, our medical officer (MO), had set up his medical base. Colonel Pip, Peter Burr and the wireless operator were put into an ambulance and set off for a Tobruk hospital.

This setback for the battalion signalled the end of the battle as far as 3RTR was concerned and although we spent the next two days receiving orders and counter-orders, there was no notable action. We were combined with 5RTR, so depleted were both battalions, and it was no surprise when we received orders to return to the delta for a rest and re-equipping.

Now followed a period of inactivity and a lot of further reorganisation. Lieutenant Colonel Roberts left the battalion on his return from hospital; he was promoted and went to command 22nd Armoured Brigade. Bob Crisp, badly wounded at Sidi Rezegh, had returned and took over command of A Squadron. I, newly promoted to captain, took over as second-in-command, still remaining as troop commander of 3 Troop.

Our new commanding officer was Lieutenant Colonel Pete Pyman, who had been GI Staff officer with 7th Armoured Division in most of the previous battles. He was therefore extremely experienced, but it was his first command at regimental level. We were somewhat apprehensive as to how he would compare with our well-loved Pip Roberts. We need not have worried. He became one of our best and trusted COs, an excellent commander and skilled tank tactician, and most considerate in his use of the tank crews. This was borne out by the fact that before the end of the war he became a major general, as did Pip Roberts too.

It was about this time that the use of 'jock columns' became popular. These were marauding armoured columns, operating independently behind enemy lines. They usually consisted of a tank squadron, a battery of twenty-five-pounders, and a motorised company of infantry. They were considered to be great fun, but obviously not liked by commanding officers as it deprived a regiment or battalion of a major part of its unit.

Nevertheless, it appealed to Bob Crisp and he immediately volunteered A Squadron to form a column. Colonel Pyman, although somewhat reluctant, agreed and so off we went.

For about eight weeks we swanned about in the desert with very little success. We did have one or two minor actions, capturing a couple of armoured cars and half-tracks with 75mm anti-tank guns. We also shot up an enemy airfield not far from El Adem.

It was during this operation that the first, certainly to my knowledge, mutinous incident happened. I was some distance away from Bob Crisp's tank when I saw it had halted. Bob and his driver were obviously having a tremendous argument. I dashed over when I saw Bob take out his revolver and was about to shoot Gillespie, his driver.

Bob was absolutely livid: 'Get back in the tank, or else. I mean it.'

'Do what you like. You can drive the bloody thing yourself. I've had enough.'

I said to Gillespie: 'Come on, you've got to get back in.' He simply shook his head.

I took Bob aside and said: 'Leave him alone. We'll have him dealt with later.'

Gillespie was sent back with a bailed-out tank crew and I understood he was court-martialled but I don't know what happened to him after that. It was an unusual occurrence, certainly in 3RTR, but understandable when you consider that Gillespie, a good driver, had already bailed out of three or four tanks whilst driving Bob Crisp. Sooner or later the bank of courage does give out.

During these rather abortive jock column operations, my own tank was again hit by a shell from a 75mm anti-tank gun. The tank caught fire, most of my crew was badly burnt and had to be evacuated. My own leg was burnt, but not too badly I thought, so I put on a shell dressing and carried on. Two or three days later my leg was in a pretty bad state and I had to be sent back. It took five days to reach a casualty clearing station, but from there I was sent to a nice hospital just outside Cairo where I spent four pleasant weeks being well looked after, followed by two weeks rehabilitation at Lady Lampson's hospice on the banks of the Nile. This was a much-envied bonus following a hospital spell, a place for officers only, with excellent food and accommodation in Lady Lampson's magnificent house. The weekly special dinner-dances attended by chosen Egyptian lovelies were the talk of Cairo.

When I returned to the battalion they were preparing to go back into the line, which was now forming at El Alamein. Once again, we were part of another formation, the 8th Armoured Brigade in the 10th Armoured Division.

Our sister regiments in the brigade were two entirely new units, the Nottinghamshire (Sherwood Rangers) and the Staffordshire Yeomanry. Both regiments had been in the Middle East for some time, stationed in Palestine, still with their horses. They were extremely well trained in cavalry procedures, raring to go, but had not seen any action. Just before they were due to join us in the desert, I was sent to Palestine with a team of NCOs to help them with their training in the use of their new tanks.

Each regiment, including 3RTR, was now equipped with two heavy squadrons of Sherman tanks and a light squadron of Crusaders. The Crusader, although a fast tank, was still only fitted with a two-pounder gun. The Sherman had a 75mm gun, untried in action as yet, but we liked the look of it and when we moved up to our concentration area behind the Alamein line, it was with a feeling of confidence.

I don't think any of us appreciated that we were approaching a critical stage in the desert campaign and that the battle of Alamein would change the fortunes of the Eighth Army.

3RTR athletics team 1938-9, Bill Close front row, second from the right.

Off duty, perhaps in Cairo, 1942. Bill Close on the right.

A pre-war commanding officer's tank crew with a Vickers medium Mk II, 1936. Bill Close on the left.

Another off-duty shot, Egypt, 1942.

A British A15 Crusader, Western Desert, 1942.

A Crusader passes a burning German Mk IV, Western Desert, 1942.

Officers of 3RTR, west of Tripoli, February 1943. Bill Close is in the middle row, fourth from the left.

A knocked-out German Tiger I, Tunisia, 1943.

An M4 Sherman from 3RTR moving up for Operation Goodwood.

A Sherman passing through a war-damaged Normandy village, 1944.

Subject:- HONOURS AND AWARDS.

3 R Tks.
Ref: D/S/7
26 Nov 44.

To:- Major W.H.Close, MC. (RTR).
c/0 152 Regt R.A.C.
GPO, Newmarket, Suffolk.

1.   The C-in-C has approved the following award.

      239070 T/Major Close.W.H. 3 R Tks. Bar to MC.

2.   You may inform your relatives, but should explain to them
that on no account may any statements be made or information
given to the Press until the King's approval to the award is
published in the Gazette.

3.   The Commanding Officer joins the Bde Comdr in congratulati
you on the above award.

B.L.A.
twc.

Lt Col.
Comdg 3 R Tks.

Letter confirming the bar to Bill Close's MC, November 1944.

(Right) Newspaper article describing the action for which Bill Close was awarded the bar to his MC.

"DOUBLE" M.C. FOR UPPINGHAM OFFICER.

Major W. H. Close, M.C., Royal Tank Regiment, only son of Mr. and Mrs. Close, 6, Newtown, Uppingham, has been awarded the bar to the Military Cross.

The citation reads as follows: "This officer commanded the leading squadron of the Battalion on the night march to Amiens on the night of 29-30 August, 1944, and entered the town despite strong enemy resistance before first light. Difficult street fighting ensued, but the determined action of this squadron lead to the penetration which allowed more tanks to be employed and resulted in the clearing of the town as far as the left bank of the River Somme. Throughout the night under exceedingly trying conditions and during the fighting on the following morning, Major Close showed the greatest determination and zeal. His personal courage was an inspiration to his squadron."

STAMFORD MEN MEET

(Below) A Sherman advancing past knocked-out German armour, Normandy, 1944.

Winter conditions for tank crew, North-West Europe, 1944-5.

A troop of Shermans advancing, winter, 1944-5.

Major Bill Close, commanding B Squadron, 3RTR, 1945.

Bill Close, ADC to General Adkins, Royal Electrical and Mechanical Engineers, Aborfield, 1953.

As adjutant, photographed in Cyprus, 1957

Lecturing on the subject of Operation Goodwood to Staff College students, 1990.

Bill Close in later life, photographed with a modern tank crew.

Bill Close in Whitehall, in 2000, being presented to the Queen.

Chapter Eleven

The Alamein Battle: Early Problems

We had been in our concentration area for a few days, getting used to our new tanks and settling in our reinforcement crews. I was having a chat with Buck Kite and Geordie Reay: 'What do you think of the Sherman?'

'Its a bit too bloody big,' said Geordie. 'The Panzer gunners and 88s will have a field day.'

Buck was also a bit apprehensive about the tank's height and thought it presented too much of a target for the German gunners. They were both pleased about the 75mm gun, with its capacity for firing both high-explosive and solid shot. They were subsequently to be proved right and we did receive many casualties when the tank 'brewed up' on being hit. The tank was rather unhelpfully nicknamed 'Tommy Cooker'.

During our many discussions on the impending battle we had been told that the balloon was likely to go up about 23 October. Sure enough, on the evening of the 23rd we moved up closer to the line. When we halted at about 9 p.m. we had advanced some eighteen miles from our concentration area to a point just in front of a massive gathering of our artillery, twenty-five-pounders and medium guns. We were also just behind our minefields.

Although we were expecting a certain amount of noise when our artillery commenced their barrage, as we were almost in amongst the guns, when the bombardment thundered down the noise and blasts were appalling. We had been ordered to stay in our tanks and stand turret watch with engines ticking over. Even with all the noise outside and inside the tanks, however, I could still hear the sound of the bagpipes as the Highland Division tried to push on through the minefield and up to the Miteiriya Ridge, which was also to be our first objective.

For an hour and a half the guns kept up their pounding; it was bright moonlight and we would see company after company of the Highland regiments advancing in line, almost as if on an exercise. Only the tremendous roar of the guns behind and the crump of shells in front marked the difference. We crouched in the turrets of our tanks, eyes straining to see what was going on. We could see the gallant Scots moving steadily on, here and there figures stumbling and finally falling flat.

Enemy machine guns swept the area and I for one was extremely grateful to have armour plating around me. There was a certain amount of solid shot whistling around but we were out of range for it to have any effect on the tanks.

Abruptly the barrage stopped. The silence was almost eerie, just the sound of the bagpipes in the distance and the occasional burst of machine-gun fire. It was a moment I shall never forget.

We were told to advance, with two lanes through the minefield to negotiate before we could open up and move on to our first objective of the ridge.

I gave orders on my radio to advance and, with 3 Troop behind me, moved slowly forward into the taped lanes that the sappers had made. I could see sappers still clearing mines on either side of us and I was being pressed by the CO to get a move on.

We had only progressed about two hundred yards when a sapper stopped me and told me that his section had practically been wiped out and the way was not cleared. Tanks were piling up behind me when Bob Crisp appeared on foot: 'What the hell is going on, Bill?'

'We can't go on, the minefield is still not cleared.' I was just as annoyed as Bob but I still didn't fancy being stuck in the minefield when daylight came. In the half light we could see the Scots still struggling to get through the minefield. We could also see the havoc that the enemy machine guns had wreaked on them: there were bodies everywhere.

The barrage opened up again, enemy aircraft dropped flares and suddenly everything seemed to happen at once. The aircraft were dropping their bombs; two landed close to my tank and rocked it on its bogies. I felt several pieces of shrapnel hit the tank and I sank a bit lower in the turret. Solid shot was also flying around and I could see several tanks to my rear had been hit, with their crews bailing out.

I was still being entreated from behind to move on but it was impossible to move out of the lanes. Things became rather confused and the chaos behind was even worse. We could only hope that the sappers would get the lanes cleared before the light came. If not, we would be in real trouble. One tank in my troop had been hit but the crew were able to bail out and safely made their way to the rear.

At last a sapper came up to me and said we could move on as they now thought they had cleared the minefield. We moved slowly up to the ridge and, with room now to disperse, were able to take on enemy targets as the light improved. The Shermans were also now able to move up onto the ridge and take on the enemy anti-tank guns that had been making life so uncomfortable for us while we were stuck in the minefield. The 75mm gun on the Sherman was now proving its worth and was working to good effect.

3RTR and the Staffordshire Yeomanry established themselves on the ridge but all attempts to push on were repulsed by concealed anti-tank guns on the reverse side of the hill and we were forced to remain in hull-down positions. We, the light squadron, were ordered out to the flank to prevent any penetration on the Shermans' positions. In any case, our two-pounders were not much use in this slugging-out battle.

The next two days, 24 and 25 October, were days of confused fighting, made even worse when a further minefield was encountered as 3RTR and the Staffordshire Yeomanry attempted to push on from the Miteiriya Ridge. This had apparently not been charted and the sappers received many casualties before eventually being able to clear it. Once again, the enemy anti-tank guns were able to take full advantage of the tanks' difficulty in getting clear of the minefield before being able to disperse, and we had many casualties.

The battle became very fluid and no real progress was made during the next few days. We had quite a number of casualties during several small skirmishes with enemy tanks, mainly from 15th and 21st panzer divisions.

On 29 October, A Squadron was sent out on its own on reconnaissance near Tel el Aqqaqir. It was believed that the German armour was concentrating nearby, but previous efforts to investigate the area had been frustrated. Several Mark III panzers operating under the cover of a number of anti-tank guns had proved particularly troublesome.

Geordie Reay, my troop sergeant, was out in front of me as we crept forward in the early morning, trying to take what cover we could among a number of derelict tanks which had been knocked out in a previous battle. We managed to get in the rear of several Mark III panzers before they spotted us and, opening fire with our two-pounders, we knocked out three or four of them.

The gunner on Geordie's tank got rather carried away – he was new to the desert – and started to fire his Besa machine gun at the enemy crews as they bailed out. He was told by Geordie to leave them alone: it was considered not done to fire on a tank crew in these circumstances.

The enemy anti-tank gunners, seeing several of their tanks in flames, realised that we were behind their position and opened up on us and, under heavy fire, we were forced to retire. We were, however, able to report the presence of part of 21st Panzer Division in position north of Tel el Aqqaqir.

The next day 8th Armoured Brigade, with 3RTR in the lead, was able to bypass Tel el Aqqaqir and set off in pursuit of the enemy panzers, which were in full retreat. The Germans were adept at their use of anti-tank gun screens and time and time again we were held up, some times for as much as a whole day.

Colonel Pyman decided that we should push on and even tried movement at night, but this proved difficult as we continually became mixed up with one or other of our sister regiments. It was also cold and wet, and we were not trained for night operations, so, although our CO requested permission to move ahead, we were told by brigade to leaguer for the night.

The next morning we continued our pursuit and the battalion caught up with retreating Italian tanks near the coast road at Galal and in a rather one-sided battle disposed of twenty tanks. Shortly after this the heavens opened and we had torrential rain for several hours. All thoughts of continued pursuit were out of the question as the desert became a complete morass and we were thoroughly bogged down.

When the chase was resumed, A Squadron in the lead with my troop in front, we found the going extremely rough in places. At one point we had to cross a narrow wadi strewn with boulders. I gave orders to Geordie

Reay to cross and take up a position on top of the ridge on the opposite side. I decided to follow on more or less the same route, but just as I reached the floor of the wadi there was an almighty bang and I found myself hanging onto the turret at a crazy angle. An anti-tank mine had blown off one of the tank tracks and a bogie wheel had collapsed. No one was hurt but the tank was completely disabled and partly blocking the route through the wadi. I immediately reported what had happened on my radio and Bob Crisp said he would try and get some sappers up to me to try and clear the way. Shortly afterwards a sapper major arrived in an armoured car and was planning to sweep round the tank when one of my crew, Trooper Evans, looking around to see if he could spot any more mines, stood on an anti-personnel mine.

These mines, called S mines, were small but quite deadly, about the size of a jam-jar, containing a charge which threw a canister in the air that exploded about waist height and scattered shrapnel. Two of my crew died instantly and the sapper major was badly wounded. I received a small wound to my left hand. Doctor MacMillan, the MO, came up in his half-track and after he'd done what he could for the others, dressed my hand. For the first time in action I felt a bit sick and nearly passed out. The doctor gave me a couple of pep pills and suggested I go back with him for a while. After a couple of hours' rest and a generous dose of medicinal whisky I rejoined the squadron, took over another tank and pressed on.

By midday 3RTR was once again outside the minefields of Mersa Matruh and, although we tried an outflanking operation, the enemy rear-guard held us off until last light. We bedded down for the night and after standing to at first light next morning, we found that the enemy had slipped away.

I was still a bit shaken from the events of the previous day, but I must say that, after weeks in the heat of the desert, I relished as never before the sight of the blue sea and the waving palms of the little resort.

Chapter Twelve

Mareth: The Left Hook

The battalion remained in the Mersa Matruh area until the end of the month, receiving some replacement crewmen and tanks to bring us up to strength. It was a very pleasant few days which we all enjoyed to the full. Daily excursions to the beach, a visit from a bath unit, and, most refreshing of all, the quartermaster was persuaded to renew our rather tatty and smelly clothing. We felt almost human again.

However, our squadron commander had departed: Bob Crisp, never one to tolerate inaction, had become somewhat bored by our enforced stay in Matruh and had somehow managed to get a lift back to Cairo. He confided to me that he needed dental treatment.

'Look after the squadron, Bill. I won't be long.'

A few days later we received the order to move further west to join up with the forces facing the El Agheila position. No Bob Crisp! When questioned about this by Colonel Pyman, my rather lame excuses carried no weight, and we moved on without him.

Alec Doig took over as squadron commander. I was a little miffed at his appointment as I had hoped to take command myself, but Alec was a most likeable officer and a first-class tank commander, in spite of the fact that most of his previous service had been with the Kenya Rifles.

Some good news did arrive whilst we were at Matruh. I learned that I had been awarded the Military Cross for my efforts at Knightsbridge and Gazala, Geordie Reay the Distinguished Conduct Medal for his bravery at Alamein, and Buck Kite the Military Medal. We managed a small celebration that night with the help of a rum issue that Geordie had somehow contrived to scrounge from the quartermaster. All very pleasant, but when we moved next morning there were one or two sore heads, including my own.

We enjoyed the luxury of moving up to our concentration area on tank transporters, quite a change for us, but it saved valuable mileage on our tracks – an important factor in the case of the Crusaders of the Recce Squadron.

I was hoping that Bob Crisp might be rejoining us at some stage, but it was not to be. He had been dismissed in some disgrace, prompting Colonel Pyman to remark, 'Crisp was my greatest asset in the desert and my biggest liability in Cairo.'

We arrived in our area around 10 March and were told that the brigade would be joining the 2nd New Zealand Division for a special task, unknown to us as yet.

Colonel Pyman called an 'O group' of all officers and we learned that a frontal attack on the Wadi Zigzag had failed, with severe casualties inflicted on the British forces. The New Zealand Division, augmented by our brigade, a KDG recce battalion, artillery and sundry supporting units – including some Free French forces under General Leclerc – were to attempt a wide 'left hook' sweep south and west by way of Foum Tatahouine.

Moving a force of 27,000 men and 6,000 vehicles, tanks and guns 350 miles through uncharted territory seemed to be a daunting task to us old hands. The tanks were to move on tank transporters as far as possible, but it was expected that, sooner or later, we would have to take to our tracks. The move was also to be conducted by night – again, as far as possible.

So it proved. The going at first was relatively easy for the transporters but later on the terrain became impossible, several transporters becoming bogged down, and we were forced to unload the tanks. Travelling at night with no lights allowed is difficult for any force, but for tanks it is a night-mare – tank commanders peering out of the turret with dust-rimed eyes, straining to maintain station with the tank in front. In order to try and observe complete secrecy, radio silence had been imposed and this made control even more difficult.

As the going became more and more difficult, by 19 March it was realised that no further progress could be made by night moves. From then on all thoughts of secrecy went by the board, so we pushed on in full daylight until contact was made at Kebeli–Gahes, where the armoured cars of the recce battalion reported enemy positions astride the road through the pass.

The light squadron was ordered to move up as near as possible to the enemy positions. I was still commanding a troop, with Buck Kite as my troop sergeant.

'Move on, Able One,' I ordered. 'Try and contact one of our armoured cars and find out what you can about the enemy positions.'

We were now moving through a narrow valley in the precipitous Gable Tabage gorge. Alec Doig was moving up with remainder of the squadron and we seemed rather bunched. I was still apprehensive about the possibility of mines.

I managed to contact one of the armoured cars, whose commander reported that the enemy position was covered by a minefield, supported by well-dug-in positions on either side of the valley in the foothills. I reported this to Alec, who relayed the message on to the CO; he ordered us to remain in observation, not to get involved and to await the arrival of the heavy squadrons.

Although I could now pick out the enemy positions, things seemed to be very quiet so I gave orders to my troop to edge forward to try and find better positions. Suddenly there was a tremendous crash and my tank started to roll over on to its side. I yelled to my crew to bail out – they needed no telling – and I was almost bypassed in the turret by my crewmen scrambling to get out. No one was hurt, but an anti-tank shell had hit us, taking off practically all the bogie wheels on one side.

I ran over to Buck's tank and told him I was taking over his tank. Very reluctantly he and his crew got out and rather miserably stood by my disabled tank until they were picked up later on.

It was obviously a well-defended position and I reported to Alec that in view of the possibility of more mines, I didn't think we could get much further on without something being done about the mines. At about 10 p.m. units of the 6th New Zealand Brigade started to move through our positions. They had field engineers with them who started to clear gaps through the minefield. I had been told on the air that B Squadron of 3RTR would be moving up to support the New Zealand infantry attack, with the Recce Squadron giving what assistance we could.

There was bright moonlight and we could see quite clearly the New Zealanders moving slowly through the minefield. They were taking casualties, men dropping here and there. B Squadron opened up with HE on the enemy defences and we on the flanks were also able to give some covering fire with our machine guns. The attack was completely successful and we were able to move up close behind the infantry, giving them support at point-blank range. Eventually we were able to establish a firm base, capturing Point 201, a vital and important feature in the enemy defences. In this attack 1,500 Italian prisoners were taken.

Nevertheless, we found the going was extremely difficult for the tanks, with large boulders and deep wadis scattered across the area, which the tank drivers found most tricky to negotiate. The whole position was well covered by excellently sited anti-tank guns on either side of the valley and several tanks in both squadrons were knocked out.

Eventually we managed to reach the high ground beyond the minefield where we were ordered to remain and give what protection we could to the New Zealanders, who were still clearing up enemy pockets of resistance.

That night was, I think, one of the most uncomfortable I had experienced. Tank crews remained at stand-by in their tanks; it was most unpleasant and bitterly cold. I did manage to get round most of the crews, telling them discretely to make themselves a brew of tea; it was forbidden to brew up inside the tank but I didn't question how they would manage it. One advantage was that I learned that Buck Kite had managed to find himself another tank and had rejoined the squadron.

A series of night attacks were carried out over the next forty-eight hours by the New Zealand infantry supported by tanks of the brigade. One such attack on the night of 24 March was carried out in brilliant moonlight by a Maori battalion supported by C Squadron of 3RTR and a squadron of Nottinghamshire Yeomanry. It was particularly successful and resulted in the capture of twenty artillery guns and anti-tank guns, with another 1,000 Italian prisoners.

Although the capture of Point 201 had given the division a secure entry into enemy positions, they still held some of the key positions on the flanks of the pass. Their artillery was particularly active and caused numerous casualties among the New Zealand infantry. Even the tank crews found it expedient to remain inside their tanks continually.

On 26 March Alec and I attended the CO's 'O group'. We were told that a concerted attack by the whole division would be made later that day. The tanks would lead the attack with all three regiments involved. We were to form up in line: Nottinghamshire Yeomanry on the right, us in the centre and the Staffordshire Yeomanry on the left. The light squadrons would be in front with New Zealand infantrymen riding on the backs of the tanks, followed by the Sherman squadrons. We were to advance 'Balaclava' fashion behind a massive artillery barrage and would also be supported by tank-busting aircraft of the desert airforce, which would be in direct wireless contact with the tank squadrons.

All this sounded terrific, but when I returned to the squadron and briefed my crews it brought forth quite a few ribald remarks, Buck Kite and Geordie Reay being particularly caustic.

We were due to commence the attack at 4 p.m. and just as we started to form up a dust storm sprang up suddenly, as they often do, making visibility rather difficult.

Our first objective was a line of defences about 1,000 yards from our start line. We reached this without any great difficulty, the German gunners still rather shaken and dazed by the barrage, making no effort to engage us. As we advanced we engaged the gun emplacements with machine-gun fire; in some cases we crushed the guns by running over them.

However, shortly after we had bypassed the first defences, the German anti-tank gunners came to life, hitting several Shermans, which burst into flames. The crack of 88mm guns and the chatter of sponsons added to the noise and chaos.

Two Crusaders on my left were hit, then I saw Geordie Reay's tank on my right hit. It ended up on its side in a concrete emplacement. Geordie's crew seemed to bail out all right and took shelter in the emplacement, no doubt relieved to be out of it for a while.

I felt a crack on the front of my tank but a reassuring yell from one of my crew confirmed that we hadn't been penetrated. Peering out of the turret I was so busy looking for targets that I failed to see a German infantryman standing up in his slit trench taking aim at me with his machine gun. My good luck was still with me: he must have been on single shot, for the first round hit the wireless mast on my tank and whined harmlessly past my head. The German was summarily dealt with by one of the New Zealanders on the back of my tank.

As we moved through the enemy defences quite a number of Italians came out of their slit trenches with their hands up. Some of the New Zealanders leapt off the tanks and went into close-contact action with their rifles and bayonets.

Alec Doig was some way to my right and seemed to be in the centre of a line of enemy anti-tank guns with their crews coming to life and starting to man their guns. I saw his tank get hit, some of his crew bailed out, but shortly after I received a message over the air that Alec had been badly wounded.

I was at last in command of the squadron, though not in the circum- stances I would have wished. We were now in the middle of the enemy defensive position. I could see terrified infantrymen cowering in their trenches, some gun crews lying still beside their guns. I became rather excited and decided to throw a few hand grenades – we suddenly had a box of six in the turret. Not having practised throwing grenades from the turret of a moving tank, I forgot that my gunner had traversed the gun. My first grenade dropped among the New Zealand infantrymen on the back of my tank and bounced off. No one was hurt, but one of the New Zealanders pointed his Sten at me, indicating what would happen should I try it again. I stuck to commanding the tank after that.

The enemy anti-tank guns were becoming more and more of a problem. Several Shermans were hit and burst into flames. Some of their crews were able to get out, but not all.

We had hoped to be able to call on the RAF Hurricanes and Kittyhawks but our observer, who had been in Alec's tank when it was hit, was also a casualty. Nevertheless, they were coming over us in waves and taking on targets to our immediate front. I only hoped that they were good at tank recognition.

At about 6 p.m. elements of the 1st Armoured Division started to move through our positions and we felt we could relax a little. The position was still very confused and although we appreciated that 1st Armoured Division were taking over the attack, 8th Armoured Brigade had orders to remain in the field more or less in open battle order.

I had been expecting orders to leaguer so that a decent meal could be brewed up and the squadron bedded down. Our casualties had been quite considerable – the light squadron had lost seven tanks, the heavy squadrons rather more. But it was not to be and we remained in our battle positions all night. At first light I was called over to Colonel Pyman's tank.

'Bill, the rear units of 1st Armoured Division are reporting that they are being attacked by panzers. Take your squadron out to the flank and find out what's going on.'

I moved out with two troops and proceeded rather cautiously towards the foothills, where I could see brilliant flashes from enemy tanks – about six or seven in good hull-down positions. I reported back to the CO and suggested that a troop of Shermans could deal with them. We would continue to engage them until the heavies came up to support us.

As we tried to tuck ourselves into some sort of hull-down position – we were still quite exposed – my troop corporal's tank was hit and burst into flames. Two members of the crew were able to bail out.

I was extremely relieved when two troops of Shermans from B Squadron came up and very quickly dealt with the enemy tanks, although not before losing three of their own.

Although we practically surrounded the enemy, pockets of determined Germans continued to fight on throughout the day until finally forced to surrender to a Maori battalion. In this particular action one of the Maori lieutenants received a posthumous Victoria Cross.

We now had a few days' rest and reorganisation in the Sfax area. Colonel Pyman left us, to go on to higher things, we were told, which indeed was true for by the end of the war he was a major general. Colonel Ian Spence, a former Staffordshire Yeomanry officer joined us as CO and a few days later we moved on to positions just short of Enfidaville, where we were to remain.

Chapter Thirteen

Enfidaville:
The End of the Desert Campaign

The approach of victory in North Africa left me with mixed emotions. Like many people who had chased or been chased up and down the desert, the idea of riding triumphantly into Tunis had its attractions. At the same time there was feeling of relief that for once we would not be in the van.

While other units went off to reinforce the First Army we hid our tanks in the shadows of the cactus thickets on the plains around Enfidaville. The mountains opposite were occupied by the 90th Light, probably the cream of the old Afrika Corps. Behind them was what was left of the 15th Panzers. I believe at that time they were considered to be part of the 5th Panzer Army but the title didn't mean anything to us.

There was still plenty of fight left in the enemy and the German and Italian infantry resisted violently when the New Zealanders attacked Takrouna, an unpleasant craggy lump of a place, and the 4th Indian Division had a go at Dejebel Garci, a mountain scored with gullies. The assault went in on the night of 19 April and all we could do was watch the flashes in the dark and the drifting smoke in the morning. The objectives were taken but at a heavy cost. The New Zealanders lost a lot of officers.

As the Recce Squadron, we were required to make several excursions into the foothills but we found little except minefields. The enemy seemed to have plenty of anti-tank guns covering them so we didn't try too hard.

When the Axis forces finally collapsed in May, I went with the CO and the other squadron leaders to watch the 90th Light surrender. I rated them second only to the 21st Panzer Division as desert fighters. I would place the 15th Panzers after them, though not without recalling the tremendous guts shown by the 88mm gunners and the Stuka crews.

The 90th marched in under their own officers and NCOs, tired and shabby and clutching what must have been their equivalent of our precious bedrolls. There was no gloating on our part, only a sense of achievement in having beaten men who, in my opinion, had fought with distinction and skill, even decency, if such a word can be applied to a battlefield.

Afterwards Colonel Spence suggested we all go and inspect the positions we'd been facing for the past fortnight and view them from the enemy side.

'Now we'll see whether our camouflage was as good as we thought it was.'

The little convoy set off in jeeps, Colonel Spence leading. We still had some way to go when I noticed we were passing some small piles of stones that looked unpleasantly like minefield markers. I signalled to the others to stop and, taking over at the wheel from my driver, drove carefully up to the CO's vehicle. Closer scrutiny confirmed my fears.

'OK, Bill, let's all go back together. Follow in my wheel tracks.'

He turned and we followed in close column, making our way slowly out of the danger area. A minute or two later there was a tremendous bang, my jeep leapt into the air and choking black smoke blotted out everything as we crashed back to earth. A series of violent explosions followed.

When the racket ceased I felt sharp pains in my head and ribs and saw, as the fumes cleared, that my driver was slumped unconscious in his seat, his ripped tunic soaked with blood. I became vaguely aware that the other jeeps had stopped and figures were making their way over. They got us out after carefully inspecting the immediate vicinity and started to bandage us.

Though my head was ringing and I was deaf for a time, I gathered the CO had driven over an Italian box mine without detonating it and that the renewed pressure of my own jeep had set it off. Several S mines had simultaneously shot up and exploded, spraying the area with ball-bearings. One had gone right through the driver's chest and out the other side. I had a nasty gash across my stomach, another at the back of my head and I wondered what other damage had been done as I was bleeding profusely.

We were now well and truly marooned. Any attempt to drive the vehicles already in the minefield out was to invite another series of blasts. Fortunately the noise attracted the attention of an armoured car which halted at a safe distance. New Zealand sappers appeared and started to clear a path. There was no way that the task could be hurried and though I was dying for a drink no one would give me one, not knowing yet the extent of my stomach wound. The most I got was a wet rag wiped over my lips and an assortment of advice and encouragement of the 'You've got a nice Blighty one there, Bill' type.

I could have done without it. Though morphine was produced from somewhere, the poor driver was in a much worse condition and it was perhaps just as well that he remained oblivious of what was going on. The mine detecting was proceeding along the old prod-with-a-bayonet lines for most of the time. It took nearly three hours to clear a path and by the time we were put on stretchers and loaded aboard some sort of vehicle, I was not particularly concerned with events.

At battalion headquarters, Doctor MacMillan took one look and packed us off to a casualty clearing station in Sfax. There it was discovered that though the ball-bearings had made a mess of the back of my head none had penetrated the skull. A single one had hit me in the back, whizzed round the outer lining of the stomach and come out again without doing serious damage. I could look forward to having two navels.

My driver, Lance Corporal Williams, was not so lucky and I heard later that he had died in hospital.

At Sfax I shared a tent in the casualty clearing station with a wounded New Zealand gunner officer called Jerry Gray. Three days after being admitted we decided we were fit enough to venture forth, so dressed and slipped out of the back of the tent and sat on the side of the Sfax road, hoping to hitch a lift into town.

'No one will miss us as long as we're back in reasonable time,' said Jerry.

We eventually managed a lift with some airmen of the American 12th Bomber Group who were in camp nearby. We had a rather riotous party in the Overseas Club in Sfax. The trouble was that by the time we had finished celebrating our liberty, we couldn't find our way back and finished the night more dead than alive in the back of one of their jeeps.

The hangover brought on by potent local liquor was even worse than the now nagging reminders delivered by our wounds. There were no flags out to welcome us.

'I had you two booked to go to 63 General Hospital in Cairo by air,' said the senior doctor, Major Morgan. 'Instead you will go to 48 General Hospital in Tripoli by road. That should cure you of your wandering habits.'

The matter didn't finish there. The escapade was reported and when I returned to duty I was called before Brigadier Baker-Baker who lectured me sternly on my responsibilities and gave me a reprimand.

I missed the big victory parade in Tunis in which the battalion took part in front of Churchill and assembled generals. My wounds kept me in hospital for six weeks and when I returned to duty, 3RTR was at Homs on the coast east of Tripoli. Our tanks had been handed over to 5RTR, soon to be in action in Sicily.

We had a good time that summer and enjoyed exploring the country without being shot at. In Tunis I bumped into Jimmy Cornwell – my old pal from sergeants' mess days – who was then commanding a squadron in 12RTR that he had helped raise from scratch. They were now part of the First Army.

He told me that after leaving Sandhurst OCTU in the winter of 1940 he'd been sent to Gateshead, where recruits were received in their civilian clothes and started their basic training in the streets without uniforms.

The battalion had seen its first action in Tunisia where it formed part of a brigade equipped entirely with Churchills. Jimmy was highly critical of the way in which the First Army had, at the start of its campaign, used tanks in penny packets and said it was not until some of the Eighth Army commanders arrived to show them how it was done that things improved.

Even so, the 12th had suffered heavy casualties, losing a complete squadron in an ugly hill fight against the Hermann Goering Parachute Regiment towards the end of April. Like me, Jimmy had been wounded on the last day of the campaign and spent some time in hospital in Algiers. When we parted I suppose we were both wondering whether the other would see out the war. By that time I had deliberately stopped cultivating new friendships as they were unlikely to last and there did not seem to be many old pals left.

The introduction of the Tiger into the North African theatre gave plenty of food for thought, though I personally had not come up against one in action. They were said to be built like battleships and when I first saw a captured specimen, which looked grim even on a sunny day undisturbed by any warlike noises, I saw what was meant. Even the side armour was thicker than the toughest part of the Sherman – the 76mm turret front. A comparison of the noses of the two tanks showed the Tiger to be twice as strong as our 50mm. I looked at the long 88 sticking from the massive turret and swallowed hard. It was quite capable of knocking out any Allied tank I knew of at about 2,000 yards, which was long before we could get near enough to do any damage. Assessment reports said the Tiger was liable to mechanical break-downs and I sincerely hoped so.

When the battalion sailed for Britain in December and the temperature began to drop I felt the outlook was distinctly what the weathermen used to call 'uncertain'.

Endnote

Years later in Cyprus I paraded before Baker-Baker in disgrace again when, now a captain, I was commanding a REME workshop unit in Famagusta. I had been reported for being in an out-of-bounds restaurant at a party thrown by one of the Turkish contractors. From the way he kept me waiting and the grim expression on his face when I entered his office, I was for the high jump. Then he looked hard at me and said, 'Oh, it's you, is it? I thought I recognised the name.' 'I'm afraid I've no excuses, sir.' 'Never mind about that,' he said. 'Did you have a good time? Come on over to the mess and you can tell me all about it.' This time there was no reprimand.

Chapter Fourteen

Homeward Bound

Our voyage home on a splendid Danish ship was more or less uneventful but nonetheless extremely pleasant. Also on board were some 200 British and Commonwealth nurses who no doubt contributed greatly to the convivial atmosphere on the ship. I was appointed black-out officer for the journey home, a job not anticipated, but which proved most interesting.

The ship was supposed to be 'dry', but the parties that went on almost non-stop throughout the voyage were certainly not dry! On my rounds as black-out officer, as a point of duty it was my privilege to have access to all cabins at any time. I was easily persuaded to turn a blind eye no matter how riotous the party.

Our only stop en route was at Sicily where we spent a pleasant two days ashore. Eventually we landed at Glasgow on Christmas Eve 1943. I had been parted from my wife Josie for just over three years, and my son Richard was now a sturdy lad, three years old.

I had three weeks' leave to come. However, during my absence Josie had joined the Auxiliary Territorial Service (ATS) so Richard was being looked after by my parents, who were still living in Uppingham. I was not particularly happy about this arrangement but did appreciate my wife's feelings about doing her bit for the war effort. Josie did manage to get a few days' leave, which we spent together, but I was not unhappy when the time came for me to rejoin the battalion.

I had learned during my leave that my promotion to major had been confirmed and that I was to retain command of A Squadron.

On rejoining the regiment I found that we were part of a new formation, the 29th Armoured Brigade within the 11th Armoured Division. A pleasant surprise was that the division was commanded by Pip Roberts, now a major general – he had commanded 3RTR in the desert in 1942. Also new was our commanding officer, Lieutenant Colonel David Silvertop, who had joined us from the 14th/20th Hussars. As tankies, we had somewhat mixed feelings about a cavalry officer ('donkey wallopers') commanding a regular tank battalion. There had always been a friendly rivalry between us, though we had no illusions about their keenness and ability.

David Silvertop was to prove to be one of our most courageous and able commanders, who gained the love and respect of everyone in the battalion. He was killed in action in tragic circumstances after we had captured Antwerp.

Our training on the Yorkshire moors was of great value, particularly to the desert veterans who found operating in entirely different terrain an enlightening experience. It also gave us the opportunity to test out our new officers and tank crews.

Most of our replacement personnel had joined us before we left North Africa. My new troop officers were Johnny Langdon, Basher Bates and Bill Yates, all ex-infantry but keen to prove their worth in a tank battalion after a short but rigorous armoured training course. This they did to great effect in the Normandy battles and the drive to the Baltic. Johnny Langdon in particular became my most trusted and courageous troop commander, remaining with me until the end of the war, gaining a Military Cross in the process.

Our first training period on the moors, Operation Eagle, was conducted in appalling weather, with snow and ice most of the time. Nevertheless, we made much of the conditions, sure that the experience would be of benefit later on in operations in Europe.

Shortly afterwards we moved south to Aldershot. The battalion was in great heart. (This was in great contrast to a report by Max Hastings in his book where he referred to the mutinous feelings of the men of 3RTR and their anti-D-Day slogans on the walls of their barracks in Aldershot. This was quite untrue and greatly resented by the battalion.)

We shared the barracks in Aldershot with one of our sister regiments in the brigade, the 23rd Hussars. This was a regiment that had been

105

revived in 1940; the men were extremely well trained and keen to show what they could do, although so far they had seen no action. The other armoured regiment in the brigade, the 2nd Fife and Forfar Yeomanry, was also well trained and raring to go, though also untried. They were to prove excellent armoured regiments in the operations to come and there is no doubt that their keenness and ability helped to keep the more experienced RTR crews on their toes.

Geordie Reay, DCM, asked to see me on interview.

'Well, Geordie, what's the beef?'

'I want to get out of the army, sir!'

It was the last thing I had been expecting. 'For what reason?'

'I don't think I am fit to command men in battle, sir. I've lost my nerve.'

I had no option but to refer the request to the CO. After hearing the same phrase about feeling unable to command men in battle, Silvertop simply said: 'I'm afraid you'll have to carry on like the rest of us, Reay.'

And so he carried on.

The 11th Armoured Division which landed across the Normandy beaches between 13 and 14 June 1944 was a powerful formation. Besides the three armoured regiments in 29th Armoured Brigade, we had the 8th Rifle Brigade (RB), which normally provided an infantry company for each armoured regiment. In addition, we had the 159th Infantry Brigade, made up of the 3 Monmouthshire Regiment, 4th Kings Shropshire Light Infantry (KSLI) and 1 Herefordshire Regiment. Divisional troops included a reconnaissance regiment, the 2nd Northamptonshire Yeomanry and 13 Royal Horse Artillery Regiment, with their twenty-five-pounder guns mounted on a tank chassis.

Our waiting in the concentration area around Southampton was incredibly boring but finally on 12 June we joined our tanks, already loaded up some days before, on the tank landing craft.

I had half my squadron on my craft, which was commanded by a bluff old Scottish skipper. The weather in the channel was at its worst, huge waves and blustery squalls making life for the tank crews perched on the top of their tanks most uncomfortable. I was rather better off, being ensconced with the skipper in his small control cabin sharing a bottle of malt whisky.

As we neared the French coast several of our flotilla turned back, thinking, no doubt, that it would be impossible to unload our tanks in the circumstances. The tanks were waterproofed but unloading them in any depth of water over three or four feet would be highly dangerous, with the possibility of the tank submerging.

My skipper was adamant – 'I'll get you there, my boy!' he said. I was not sure at this stage whether I was pleased or not. He was as good as his word and he got us close into shore where we were able to unload with no problems. I was also very pleased to see that the other craft with the remainder of my squadron were also able to get ashore.

The beach by this time was fairly well organised and we were able to make our way inland to our rendezvous area. Only half the regiment managed to get ashore that day and it was two or three days later before the remainder of the battalion caught up with us.

Chapter Fifteen

Operation Epsom: The Battle for Hill 112

Caen had been the D–Day objective of 3rd Infantry Division, following its landing on Sword Beach. But, faced by the opposition of 21st Panzer Division, the city had proved to be a step too far. Generals Montgomery (21st Army Group) and Dempsey (Second British Army) wished to avoid having to launch an inevitably costly street battle for Caen. If Dempsey could outflank it, and break through onto the high ground astride the Caen–Falaise road, the German positions around Caen would become untenable. Launched at the end of June in the area a few miles west of Caen, Operation Epsom was planned to achieve this.

The 15th (Scottish) Infantry Division was to strike south, drive a wedge between the German positions in the area of Cheux and push on south to cross the River Odon near Baron. 11th Armoured Division would then pass through, cross the Orne and reach the high ground beyond.

It was to be the division's first taste of battle, and was to be fought in country very different from the open desert which Bill Close and 3RTR had experienced in North Africa. The 'bocage' country, consisting of small fields, surrounded by high banks surmounted by thick hedges, and interlaced with sunken roads and lanes, was ideal defensive country. Tanks felt very vulnerable to short-range weapons. Calling for artillery fire support was impossible when the target was only about one to two hundred yards ahead.

The attack was launched on 26 June. In the face of strong German defence, progress was slow and costly. 29th Armoured Brigade managed to cross the Odon and secure a foothold on Hill 112, but, in the face of strong counterattacks by several German panzer divisions which were rushed to the area, the brigade was withdrawn. By the beginning of July it was evident that Operation Epsom had failed in its attempt to outflank Caen.

*   *   *

Our first few days in Normandy were uneventful, our tanks tucked away in typical Normandy orchards, crews relaxing, the peace only marred by the bloated corpses of rotting cows – the stench was awful.

We learned that our first task was to try and capture the bridges over the Odon, with 15th Scottish Division to be the spearhead of the attack. Their first objective was to capture the village of Cheux. This was quite strongly held and the Scots took particularly heavy casualties: when 3RTR moved through the ruins of the village the ground was littered with dead infantrymen.

Our task was to push on to Evercy and on to the Orne, an advance of almost twenty miles. In the end, only five miles were gained. Most of the trouble came from anti-tank fire from the wooded slopes of Hill 112 and the slightly larger Hill 113. Several tanks were knocked out, C Squadron being particularly badly hit.

The wooded country in the valley of the Odon was an obstacle in itself, tending to produce confusion amongst the tank formations, which were further handicapped by the narrowness of the attack frontage limiting the deployment of the total tank strength. Our sister regiment, the 23rd Hussars, did however succeed in reaching the Odon, where a bridge was captured intact.

Next day the 23rd Hussars forged their way forwards, reaching the flat-topped crest of Hill 112 overlooking the village of Esquay. Later that day they were driven off the crest by fire from several Tiger tanks well dug-in in the woods on the far slope.

In the afternoon we received orders from Colonel Silvertop that we were to relieve the 23rd Hussars on the hill – a rather daunting proposition, as we moved through some of the burnt-out tanks of the Hussars.

A Squadron was to lead 3RTR and I moved on with Johnny Langdon's troop as point troop. Geordie Reay was his troop sergeant. Like many desert veterans, Geordie felt uneasy in this land of small fields and wooded areas, with ditches and hedgerows ideal ambush positions for bazooka men. He was quite relieved when his tank broke down with a mechanical fault, but then a little taken aback when ordered to take over his troop corporal's tank. It was an unwritten rule in 3RTR that an NCO stayed with his tank until it was repaired. However, I wanted Reay to continue in his role of troop sergeant as his experience was invaluable.

We had our faithful G Company of the 8 RB with us, moving closely behind us. It gave us great confidence to know that they would be holding the bridgehead to our rear. We had trained with them in Yorkshire and knew them intimately, squadron commander working with company commander. My own A Squadron usually seemed to work with G Company, commanded by Noel Bell, a liaison which proved to be most successful and was to continue right through to the Baltic.

I gave orders to Sugar One, Johnny Langdon's troop, to push on in an attempt to get into the village of Baron, slightly beyond the crest of the hill. As he moved forward his troop came under intense fire from enemy tanks already ensconced in the village. One tank was lost in the process as it burst into flames. It seemed as if we were exposed to fire from three directions, both from Tiger tanks and 88mm flak guns. I asked permission to pull back to slightly less exposed positions, but from where we could still engage the enemy.

We remained in these rather negative positions for the remainder of that day. We were able to knock out several anti-tank guns but could not make any impression on the dug-in Tiger tanks. We remained in position on this hill for thirty-six hours. That first night was most unpleasant; we more or less stood to in our tanks as we knew we were practically surrounded, our one consolation being that we were under the protection of the Rifle Brigade.

At first light there seemed to be a slight relapse in enemy fire and we were rather surprisingly able to 'brew up' a welcome breakfast. Shortly afterwards we were subjected to a tremendous barrage of mortar bombs ('Moaning Minnies') – a multi-barrelled weapon which could fire bombs containing from 70 to nearly 300 pounds of explosive. Though not particularly dangerous to tanks, they were lethal to infantry. Most of us were out of our tanks and we lost several NCO tank commanders and crewmen before we could take cover, Sergeant Percy Brett, another one of our desert veterans, being one of the casualties.

I managed to scramble hastily into our tank with my crew and I could see that most of the squadron were doing the same. I gave orders for the squadron to disperse; we were far too concentrated and obviously presenting a splendid target for the mortars, who had the range down to a tee.

Colonel Silvertop gave orders over the air for me to move A Squadron out to the left flank of the crest to try and get established in the village of Esquay. Just as we moved off another salvo of Moaning Minnies arrived, one landing on the back of my tank. For one dreadful moment I thought it was going to join me in the turret. Flames arose from the back of the tank and I gave orders to bail out. The crew needed no encouragement – I think one of the worst fears a tank man has is of being trapped in a burning tank.

I darted over to one of my HQ tanks and started to transfer my kit, maps, etc., when I noticed that the fire on my tank had subsided. On inspection I found that it was only the bedrolls on the back of the tank that had caught fire, the bomb had not even penetrated the engine covers. Rather sheepishly my crew and I got back in the tank.

Moving up into position between my two leading troops, I found they were being engaged from all directions. Bill Yates' troop on my left had lost two tanks and was unable to get further forwards.

'Hello Sugar Two. Tuck yourself away and give supporting fire as we move forward,' I said over the air.

'Sugar One. Try and get into cover on your right, enemy tanks to your front.'

Johnny pushed forward and managed to find a bit of cover from some small trees and started to engage the Tigers to his front. Suddenly Geordie Reay's tank erupted into a pillar of flame and smoke. I saw Geordie and one of his crew bail out, both with clothes burning and obviously wounded. I ran over to them. Geordie and his gunner Rowley were both badly burnt and I didn't have much hope for their survival. The lower part of the tank had taken the 88mm shell and the remainder of the crew was dead.

Shortly afterwards a Rifle Brigade half-track arrived and we put Geordie and his gunner on board. I learned afterwards that the half-track was hit by a shell and Geordie was wounded again in both arms. Some time later I was on leave in the UK and visited Geordie in hospital. He was still receiving skin grafts, had lost both ears and part of his nose, one hand was missing and the other was crippled, but he was still irrepressible and full of hope for the future.

Later that morning we enjoyed some success. The Rifle Brigade, with support from 3RTR, cleared the small wood on the southern slope of Hill 112. Luckily, most of the enemy had withdrawn from their positions and we had relatively small casualties.

It was hoped that we might be able to resume our drive to the Orne, but we received orders to pull back across the bridges of the Odon. Perhaps there was some feeling of disappointment in the division that we were not able to proceed, but I think there were few from 3RTR who regretted leaving Hill 112.

We were rather concerned about the retreat off the hill. There was only a narrow corridor behind us, but with our trusty Rifle Brigade holding the small bridgehead secure the move was conducted without further loss.

We lost about ten tanks on Hill 112, five of them in my squadron alone. Apart from our casualties in men, I was somewhat irritated by the loss of my bedroll in the blaze on my tank.

It was the first action with the 8th Rifle Brigade and it certainly cemented the regard we had for each other. Reputations had been gained in the battle and most of our new tank commanders and crews acquitted themselves with great credit. However, it was not so within the higher echelons, for we learned that the divisional commander, General Pip Roberts, had occasion to sack the brigadier commanding 159th Infantry Brigade and two battalion commanders were also replaced – this, after only twenty-four hours of battle. It only goes to show that exercises on the Yorkshire moors are no substitute for actual battle and there is no telling how men will behave under fire.

For a few days following Hill 112 we were split up, serving with different units, but later on we reformed as a division and went into reserve. This gave us an opportunity for a few days' rest and reorganisation before heading for the 'sharp end' again.

Chapter Sixteen

Operation Goodwood, Part I

Operation Goodwood, which took place some six weeks after D–Day, was the largest tank battle in which British troops have ever taken part. Following the failure of all attempts to force the Germans to give up Caen without the need for a direct assault on the city, it was eventually accepted that a head-on attack must be launched. Caen was finally taken on 9 July. Following its fall, General Montgomery was at last poised to launch the break-out from the Normandy beachhead.

Throughout June the Germans had been trying desperately to withdraw their panzer divisions from 'ground-holding' roles, in order to concentrate them for a massive, co-ordinated attack against the Americans. By early July 1st SS and 12th SS panzer divisions had at last been pulled back to the Falaise area. The success of Montgomery's plan required that they should, once again, be sucked into the battle to contain the British in the east, thereby allowing the Americans to launch the major break-out in the west against weaker opposition. Montgomery's plan therefore involved a two-phase attack.

In the east General Dempsey was to launch General O' Connor's VIII Corps, consisting of three armoured divisions, in an attack south from the bridgehead east of the River Orne, which had been captured on D-Day by 6th Airborne Division. The aim was to break through to the high ground astride the Caen–Falaise road. If all three armoured divisions could be brought quickly into line abreast, the pressure on the German defences in the area would be immense. They would need to deploy all available tanks to have any hope of containing the advance. Three days later General Bradley would launch the break-out, Operation Cobra, in the west, against much weaker opposition.

But there was a problem. The bridgehead east of the Orne, from which VIII Corps would attack, was very narrow initially. General Roberts' 11th Armoured Division would lead, followed, in series, by Guards and 7th

Armoured divisions. As the area widened out in the area of Cagny, 11th Armoured would swing south-west, Guards Armoured would come up on their left and swing south-east towards Vimont, and, when sufficient space allowed, 7th Armoured would provide the central thrust of this trident, driving south. For 11th Armoured speed was essential so that the following divisions could come up into line as quickly as possible. To help the initial advance the attack would be preceded by a huge artillery and air bombardment.

At only 2,000 metres wide initially, there was room for only one armoured regiment to lead. This 'privilege' was given to 3RTR, with Bill's A Squadron leading on the right and Jock Balharrie's B Squadron on the left. After crossing the Caen–Troarn railway line the ground began to open out; 2nd Fife and Forfar Yeomanry would come up on 3RTR's left, with 29th Armoured Brigade's advance continuing, therefore, on a two-regimental front heading south-west towards their objectives, the villages along the Bourgebus Ridge.

Based on the intelligence picture painted, expectations for success were high. However, intelligence had led the attackers to believe that the German defences were only about five miles deep, and to consist largely of infantry, exhausted after six weeks of continuous fighting. It was considered that there were likely to be no German tanks within about ten miles. Unaccountably intelligence had missed the fact that the defences were actually ten miles deep, with a regiment of Mark IV and Tiger tanks on the east flank, a battalion of fifty self-propelled anti-tank guns in the centre, and a line of forty-four 88mm anti-tank guns along the dominating ground of the Bourgebus Ridge. All of these could knock out a Sherman tank from 2,000 yards range, while the Sherman's 75mm gun, effective at not more than about 1,200 yards range, could not penetrate the Tiger's hide. Attacking an enemy who is well sited and well concealed on the dominating ground, and whose weapons out-range and out-penetrate you must be a terrifying business. Bill's description of the battle should be seen in this context.

Goodwood was launched on 18 July and although 11th Armoured managed to reach the slopes of the Bourgebus Ridge by late morning, all attempts to take the key villages of Bras, Hubert-Folie and Bourgebus failed. Following closely behind, Guards Armoured swung left, and met strong opposition from the German tanks. The clutter of vehicles made it impossible for 7th Armoured to come up into line between them. By evening VIII Corps was firmly held, well short of its objectives. During the night of 18/19 July the Germans rushed forward their panzer divisions.

By the end of the battle, 8th Corps had lost over 400 tanks, but the successful attack on Bras, by the few remaining tanks of 3RTR and infantrymen of 8th Rifle Brigade on the afternoon of 19 July, was the critical event, which secured the first 'toe-hold' on the Bourgebus Ridge. Tactically Operation Goodwood was something of a disappointment, since it did not penetrate as far as had been hoped. But, by the end of the battle, six and a half panzer divisions were in the line confronting the British, some 650 tanks, allowing the Americans in the west to launch their break-out against just one and a half panzer divisions of only 150 tanks. Strategically Goodwood was a significant success.

Hill 112, our first action in Normandy, had quite a salutary effect on the battalion. We had received quite a bloody nose in the battle, losing a number of our men and tanks, but on the plus side, the new crews had gained valuable experience.

Following a few days' rest all crews were in good heart and we felt we were ready for the next task. We took part in a minor operation supporting 32nd Guards Brigade in an abortive attack against the Germans on Carpiquet airfield. It was called off after forty-eight hours and we rejoined the division in a semi-rest area in the orchards around the village of Ranville just west of the River Orne.

About 10 July, at Colonel Silvertop's O group, we were warned to prepare ourselves for a major operation. Tank crews were to get as much rest as possible as the preliminary part of the operation would possibly entail two night marches. We learned that the division was to spearhead an armoured attack over the Orne, with two other armoured divisions also taking part: 11th Armoured Division would lead, followed by the Guards Armoured Division and then the 7th Armoured Division.

Because of the small size of the bridgehead over the Orne, the armoured divisions would have to go one at a time, and to observe as much secrecy as possible, the approach marches would have to be carried out overnight – not the ideal way to prepare for a major battle. Even then it was only possible for the leading division to be over the Orne when the operation started and the armoured brigade could not be moved over the river until the very night before the operation commenced.

At my CO's O group I had learned that 3RTR were to lead the attack, with my A Squadron on the right, B Squadron on the left and C Squadron in reserve. Other details we learned were that the operation would be preceded by a massive air bombardment by British and American aircraft, followed by a rolling barrage behind which the tanks would advance.

When I briefed my squadron crews there were quite a few caustic comments from some of the old hands, with reminders of the last time the battalion had taken part in a Balaclava-type charge at Mareth in the desert. My only comment, for consolation, was the fact that we would be in the front, possibly the best place to be by far. I don't think this went down particularly well.

As anticipated, our night moves proved to be horrendous, moving nose to tail along dusty winding tracks, tank commanders peering with bleary eyes out of their turrets, trying to maintain station on the tank in front. I had warned my commanders of the dire consequences should anyone doze off before we reached our first concentration area. However, this first move on the night of 16/17 July was accomplished without undue incident and we arrived in an area just west of the Orne about 1 a.m.

Our orders were to lie up for the day, camouflage our tanks and get as much rest as possible. However, the guns and instruments in the tanks had to be cleaned to remove the appalling dust that covered everything after the night march. We were able to cook meals on our small tank stoves, although no fires were allowed and all movement was to be kept to a minimum in the leaguer area. During the day we received our first delivery of mail, papers and beer since landing in Normandy. We found the beer a welcome relief from the copious quantities of cider and Calvados which everyone had been consuming – wreaking, I am sure, untold damage to the inner man.

At 4 p.m. I attended Colonel David's O group to learn the order of attack and to study some excellent-quality photographs of all the villages and enemy positions in the line of our advance. Although we reckoned the countryside over which we were to advance seemed to be good tank

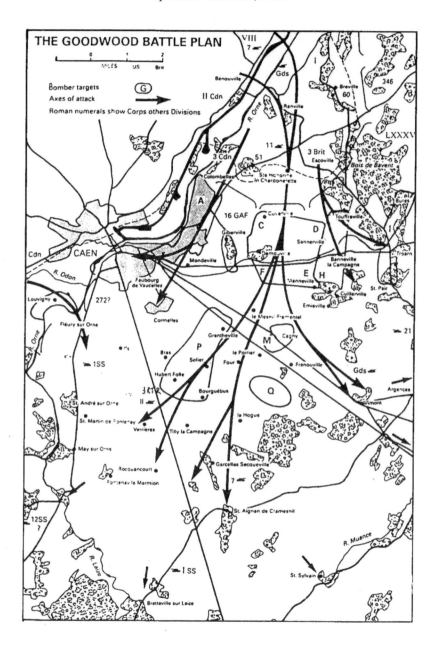

The Goodwood Battle Plan

country – and we were pleased to be away from the close bocage – it also proved to be good tank-killing country.

On the night of 17/18 July we made our second move, starting off about 10 p.m., again nose to tail, rather like the circus coming to town.

Again the dust was dreadful and I was glad that I had chosen to lead with my tank. After several scares when odd tanks strayed out of the taped lanes, we eventually crossed the Orne and moved into our final concentration area just behind the start line at about one o'clock in the morning. The area was a mass of crashed gliders of the 6th Airborne Division who had taken the bridgehead on D-Day. We had also been told, rather belatedly, that just in front of our start line one of our own minefields had only been cleared the night before, with four lanes through it.

After instructing my crews to prepare their tanks for battle and get a brew if possible, Noel Bell, commanding G Company, 8 RB, and I walked down to the minefield to recce the taped lanes which we hoped would be well signed. There seemed to be no problem – the entrances to the minefield were guarded by immaculately dressed provost NCOs, all white belts and gaiters. I didn't think we would have any difficulties in getting through the minefield, but I was still a little apprehensive about what we would look like at first light, lining up in full view of the enemy. We had orders to form up in three waves: first wave – A and B squadrons; second wave – Regimental HQ, recce troop, Carrier Platoon, 1 Troop Flails, half troop Armoured Vehicle Royal Engineers (AVRE)s; third wave – Reserve Squadron, Motor Company, 13 Royal Horse Artillery.

On my return to my squadron I found my crew had managed to make a brew and they were trying to get their heads down for a while. It would be an early start with first light about 4.30 a.m.

Just before first light we moved slowly down to the minefield nose to tail, closely followed by the carrier platoon of G Company commanded by David Stileman. As expected, we had no difficulties in negotiating the taped lanes through the minefield although one of the carriers did stray out of its lane and lost a track on a mine.

Sure enough, as we formed up on the start line as the light came, my fears were well founded: a complete regimental group concentrated in such a small area must have presented a considerable target to the enemy.

Strangely enough, however, no enemy fire was directed at us at that time and we busied ourselves with last-minute battle preparations.

A minute to go. Under a dark sky with the dust drifting, the Shermans waited, engines throbbing, radios crackling. Owing to the close proximity of the tanks, only a few yards apart, the radio operators were having difficulties in netting in their sets. This was to cause some problems in control later on.

We had been sitting on our tanks since about 5.45 a.m., watching the armada of planes saturating the area in front of us. All the villages had been absolutely plastered with heavy-calibre bombs, resulting in enormous explosions and eruptions over the whole area, which we heartily cheered. We thought nothing could survive such an onslaught, but how wrong we were.

A few figures stood about enjoying a final cigarette – they should have been in their tanks! At 7.45 a.m. on the dot the barrage came down, some 200 guns firing on a front of 2,000 yards immediately ahead of us with others concentrating on targets further back.

Rrrr, flash, wham! Rrrr, flash, wham!

One of our batteries dropped a salvo right among us and a figure dashed over to my tank.

'It's Mr Pells, sir, he's had it!'

Philip Pells, 3 Troop commander, had been caught out of his tank. I told his troop sergeant, Freddie Dale, to take over the troop. He was an experienced sergeant and well able to cope. There were several other casualties, including Peter Burr, C Squadron commander, killed.

By the time we had seen to our casualties the barrage had started to creep forwards. We had orders to try and remain 100 yards behind but we set off in some disorder.

Straining my eyes from the open turret I took some comfort that the rest of the Second Army was right behind us and if it wasn't, it ought to be. About 100 yards ahead, geysers shot up above the murk, the barrage thundering on, slinging clods in its wake.

The mayhem had begun at 5.45 a.m., when the hundreds of bombers had dropped their loads on the countryside. Everyone had a go that morning – RAF, Yanks, the navy (the monitors lying off Arromanches had let fly with their fifteen-inch guns). The artillery was supposed to put the finishing touch to the general pandemonium.

We roared on through boiling clouds of dirt and fumes, thirty-eight Shermans doing their best to keep up with the rolling curtain of fire. I could vaguely see tanks on either side of me slowly picking their way through the ever-increasing number of bigger and bigger bomb craters. I only hoped that B Squadron on my left was also keeping up. As Peter Burr had been lost at the start, it was now up to Jock Balharrie, B Squadron commander, and myself. I kept willing us on.

Dazed and shaken figures rose from the uncut corn and attempted to give themselves up to the leading tanks. When I waved them to the rear they stumbled off with their hands over their ears. Other Germans squatted in their foxholes staring stupidly, completely demoralised as we passed. Our infantry would collect them, or so we hoped. Sure enough, we could see David Stileman's carriers rounding them up and escorting them to the rear.

As we moved slowly forwards, with engines whining as drivers changed down in order to bypass the still-smoking bomb and shell craters, the barrage drew further away. We were now able to open up a bit, visibility was a bit better, and I now had my squadron more or less in line, covering a frontage of about 600 yards. I gave instructions to 1 Troop commander, Johnny Langdon: 'Sugar One, move out to your right. Anti-tank guns firing from the orchard area; use your machine guns to keep their heads down.'

I wanted to slow down a bit and deal with them properly but with instructions from the CO to press on, we could only 'brass them up'. Ahead of us lay the Caen–Troarn railway line. It had a small embankment but I didn't think it would cause any problems for the tanks. So it proved: the tanks had no difficulties, though when I approached it myself, I foresaw trouble for the soft-skinned vehicles of the rear echelons and called up the sapper AVREs to blow holes in the embankment.

We knew that the barrage was due to halt at the line of the railway, but before we had gathered ourselves in some sort of order it moved and we set off in pursuit. As we moved up a slight slope towards the village of

Le-Mesnil-Frementel odd rounds of solid shot started whistling by – obviously the first signs of organised resistance. Suddenly a Sherman on my left rolled to a halt, belching smoke. Immediately, every tank turned its guns on the houses in the village from where the shot had come.

I could see considerable activity among the trees in the orchard and flashes from anti-tank guns in the line of hedgerows around the orchard. Two more tanks from the recce troop were hit before the concentrated fire from the Shermans quickly dealt with our attackers, knocking out three or four guns and their crews.

I could see that B Squadron on my left had also had two tanks hit as they were blazing furiously. Hatches flew open. Dark shapes rolled on the ground. The corn caught fire.

By this time the second regiment in the brigade, 2 Fife and Forfar Yeomanry, had come up on our left and their reserve squadron also came under heavy anti-tank fire from the village of Cagny. The squadron lost practically all its tanks in a matter of moments.

I was told in no uncertain terms to get a move on, to bypass Le-Mesnil-Frementel, and advance on to the next village of Grentheville, some 1,500 yards to my front. I was somewhat reluctant to present the flanks of my tanks to an obviously well-defended village, but gave orders to my troops to fire on the move as we passed to the west of the village.

It was now plain that although a wide strip of the country had been devastated – splintered trees and dead cows were everywhere – the enemy was present in much greater depth than we had been led to expect. Ahead lay more villages and undamaged woods, more 88s and 75s, both towed and self-propelled, and for all we knew Tigers and Panther tanks could be lurking. What was also painfully obvious was that the dazed and shaken enemy was coming to life. Earlier we had heard talk of it being 'good tank country' – largely bare of cover – a day at the races! Now the odds didn't look so promising. Runners and riders were coming unstuck at an alarming rate. It was only ten o'clock. God help My Boy Willie.

So far A Squadron had had an easy passage, with only one casualty, but as we approached Grentheville I could see the crews of anti-tank guns feverishly swinging their weapons towards us. *Nebelwerfer* bombs howled overhead; there were some twenty or thirty gun positions out in

121

the cornfields in front of the village. I gave orders for all tanks to brass them up with their machine guns or to simply run over them with their tracks.

Woompf! A Sherman right next to me burst into flames and two more were ablaze within minutes. Hatches flew open and more crews came tumbling out to roll in the corn. B Squadron on my left was also receiving an alarming number of casualties.

It was only too obvious that we would have to find some cover from fire and get some artillery fire down on the village. To my right, running north and south, was the Caen–Bourgebus railway. It had a steep embankment and I told my troop commanders to tuck themselves in along the embankment and get as much fire as they could onto the northern edge of the village.

Johnny Langdon and Buck Kite had lost two tanks each from their troops but managed to get into cover along the embankment close by my tank. Buck started to engage the enemy anti-tank guns with his seventeen-pounder gun and succeeded in knocking out two very quickly. Shortly afterwards he reported that he had hit and burnt out two self-propelled (SP) guns. These were large vehicles with either an 88mm or 105mm gun on board.

From the outset of the attack I had a gunner from 13 Royal Horse Artillery, our mobile artillery, acting as an observer – an OP or observation post – in a sawn-off Honey tank.

I called him over to me: 'Hello OP, for Christ's sake get some artillery fire down on the village as quick as you can.'

It was the first chance we had to bring our artillery into action. Within a matter of minutes the twenty-five-pounders were in action to great effect and life became a little more bearable.

Colonel Silvertop came on the air: 'Bill, get your squadron over to the west side of the embankment.'

There were two ways to do this; either crawl over the embankment or use the openings where the road and the Caen–Vimont railway went under the embankment. I chose the latter and gave instructions to my leading two troops to move under. No one moved so I stood up in my tank, waved my beret around my head and said over the air: 'Conform to me!'

As I shot under the embankment, rather like a rat up a drainpipe, I had a sudden thought: 'I hope to God there are no mines.' All was well and I emerged on the western side into perfectly peaceful-looking countryside. The two remaining squadrons gave covering fire as the rest of my squadron came through and joined me. Eventually the whole of the regimental group passed through and deployed on the western side of the embankment.

We had received a considerable number of casualties, with seven tanks knocked out from my squadron and a similar number from B and C squadrons. I had lost another troop commander, Bill Yates, so another troop sergeant, Sergeant Mason, had to take over temporary command of the troop.

It was now about 11 a.m., and our objectives, the villages of Hubert–Folie and Bras on the Bourgebus Ridge, lay ahead of us – observing through our binoculars, it didn't seem as if they were occupied. Once again we were to be proved wrong.

I had moved with my squadron out to the right flank just short of the Cormelles factory area which, as far as I was aware, was still held by the enemy. Johnny Langdon reported that a panzer tank, probably a Mark IV, was starting to move out from the factory buildings. It was swiftly dealt with by the troop.

The battalion was now more or less in line, in fairly open country with very little cover, the whole area a mass of waving golden corn that was so high that the carriers of David Stileman's platoon could barely be seen. Only the commander showed above it.

We moved slowly up the hill towards our objectives, the villages on the ridge, occasionally stopping to peer through our binoculars. Still no sign of the enemy. When we were about 500 yards from the two villages, all hell broke loose and we came under intense fire from all directions: Bras and Hubert-Folie, even from across the railway embankment and Bourgebus.

Immediately, tanks in all three squadrons were hit, bursting into flames with crew members tumbling out and the corn blazing all around.

In a matter of moments the peaceful-looking countryside was transformed into what might have been an artist's impression of a battlefield.

Except this was no artist's impression – this was for real. Burning tank crews bailed out and rolled in agony on the ground. Crew members carried their more seriously wounded comrades away from the burning tanks. Half tracks and carriers of the Rifle Brigade came up to the tanks and helped to get crewmen out where this was at all possible.

Wham! Crash! My own tank was hit and a stentorian yell emanated from down below: 'Bail out, sir!' I needed no telling and my crew joined me. No one was hurt and the tank had not caught fire, so I waved them back to the embankment area where the CO had set up his HQ. I dashed over to one of my HQ tanks and was rather disconcerted to find it had also been knocked out, the crew having already bailed out.

My troop corporal's tank was still in commission, so, having turned out its commander, I carried on command of what was left of my squadron from this tank. Both B and C squadrons had also been badly hit, losing more than half of their tanks. There was no doubt now that the villages on the hill were strongly held!

It was still important to try and get into the villages and I had orders for individual tanks to find what cover we could and bring some fire down on the forward edges of the villages. My faithful gunner OP was still close by me so I called him over and told him to get some artillery fire down on both villages as quickly as possible.

Together with Buck Kite's two tanks, I managed to find a small dip in the ground with a few small trees and shrubs, which afforded some cover from sight at least. We managed to get into hull-down positions and proceeded to engage enemy anti-tank gun positions in both villages. We could also see that there were several enemy tanks on the ridge, probably Panthers. I gave orders for Buck Kite to move round to the right of Bras, taking with him his Sherman seventeen-pounder, one of the few still in action. The move was successful and he succeeded in knocking out two Panthers trying to outflank us from the west.

My own gunner, Todd, was also having some success and managed to knock out a couple of anti-tank guns on the forward edge of Bras. I was still concerned about getting onto the ridge and instructed Johnny Langdon to try and move up between the two villages. This he managed

124

to do and reached the road connecting them but both of his tanks were hit. Johnny and his crew bailed out unhurt and he was able to take over his troop corporal's (Corporal Killeen) tank.

B and C squadrons were also heavily engaged trying to move forward but losing tanks all the time. It was only too obvious that we could not advance without sustaining further casualties. Realising this, the CO ordered us to pull back to rather negative positions while continuing to engage all visible targets.

We were also getting low on ammunition and petrol. A couple of replenishment lorries managed to get forward and tanks were able to pull back one by one to refuel and take on more ammunition.

Regimental HQ down by the embankment was being rather heavily bombarded by artillery fire and it was not until one of the Rifle Brigade sergeants wandering along the embankment found a German observer well dug into the side of the railway – who he summarily dealt with him – that things became a little quieter.

For the rest of the day we stayed in these rather negative positions, unable to get forward. Just before last light four Panther tanks advanced over the ridge towards our positions. Two were quickly knocked out, forcing the other two to retreat back to Bourgebus.

And so ended a somewhat exhausting and frustrating day; so near and yet so far from our objectives. We leaguered down by a quarry near the embankment. During the night there was some shelling and one or two enemy bombers ranged the area. This made for a disturbed few hours with little chance of sleep. Some replacement tanks and crews came up during the night; most of the crewmen had bailed out during that first day. I was pleased that I still had Johnny Langdon with me as most of my other officers had become casualties during the day.

Bernard Hammill, my second-in-command, had also been knocked out earlier in the day and was seriously wounded. However, with the additional replacement tanks and crews, the battalion was able to re-organise into three squadrons of ten tanks each. B Squadron commander, Jock Balharrie, had also been knocked out and slightly wounded, but joined us later on.

I was still rather fortunate in having my two experienced troop sergeants, Buck Kite and Freddie Dale, fit and well, although I don't think that any of us were looking forward to the next day with any great enthusiasm. The Bourgebus Ridge with its strongly held villages seemed a daunting task for our depleted forces.

Chapter Seventeen

Operation Goodwood, Part II

After a somewhat disturbed night with very little chance to get my head down, I reported to Colonel David's tank at about 4.30 a.m., just before first light, to get orders for the day. There was little change in them: our objectives were the same. Hubert-Folie and Bras on the ridge were our target.

Of some consolation was the information that at least two medium artillery regiments had managed to come forward and could be available to assist in our attacks. Also, our infantry brigade was now available to come forward, following its rather abortive attempts to subdue the villages at Culverville and Demoville further back.

As we pushed out from the leaguer, my orders to my tank commanders were brief but to the point: 'We have to get into the villages on the ridge.' Try not to get involved, the CO had said, tongue-in-cheek.

As we moved up towards Bras I could see that there were more enemy tanks in excellent hull-down positions between the villages and out to the west of Bras. Once again I took Buck Kite's three tanks with me out to the right flank and attempted to get round the western edge of the village. We got to within about 400 yards of the first houses when once more we were subjected to heavy anti-tank fire – from the village, from Panther tanks and also from the village of Ifs, out to the west. Immediately two of Buck's tanks were hit and I could see that several other tanks from B and C squadrons were also hit and blazing furiously.

I had also given Johnny Langdon's troop the task of trying to push forward between the two villages. Once again he gallantly led his tanks across the track connecting the villages, knocking out two Panthers in the process, before once again losing two of his tanks, including his own. I could see several of his crew members trailing back through the corn, carrying some of their more seriously wounded comrades.

I gave orders to pull back into some sort of cover and, calling over my gunner OP, told him to get the artillery on to both villages as quickly as possible. B and C squadrons were also in trouble and pulling back to the line of the railway embankment, which did afford some protection.

I managed to tuck myself, along with Buck Kite's Sherman seventeen-pounder, into a dip in the ground about 500 yards from the northern edge of Bras, where we were able to engage the Panthers that were attempting to outflank us. Two Panthers were quickly knocked out by Buck's seventeen-pounder. My own gunner was also doing sterling work, accounting for two SP guns which were engaging us from the western edge of Bras.

We were once again completely pinned down by the extremely accurate anti-tank fire from all directions. It was obvious that both villages were strongly held and the presence of more Panzers on the ridge made our position untenable. I reported this to Colonel David who gave orders for us to sit tight and to try and hold off the enemy tanks. In the meantime, he would try and get the RAF to make a strike on the ridge. We knew we had a cab-rank of Tiffies (RAF Typhoons) above us somewhere, but, having lost our RAF liaison officer early on in the battle, they had not been as effective as we had hoped.

I called up my gunner OP and told him to get some artillery fire down as quickly as possible on both villages. This he was able to do and things became a little quieter. Shortly afterwards, several tank-buster planes swooped down and attacked the Panther tanks to our immediate front, knocking out two, and the remainder then pulled back off the ridge.

We remained in these rather negative positions, for whenever we tried to move forward we lost another tank. I now had only five tanks left, including my own; B and C squadrons were also in about the same state. The day wore on slowly. It was extremely hot in the tank and I was a little worried that we were running out of both ammunition and petrol.

At about 3 p.m. I was called back to RHQ to receive new orders. As I moved back to the embankment area, several planes came streaking down the line of the embankment. They were the first we had seen. They made life very uncomfortable for a few moments before taking off southwards.

At Colonel David's O group we were told that a concerted attack was to be made on Bras and Hubert-Folie. At 4 p.m. the Northants Yeomanry, our recce regiment, would attack Bras with the H and F companies of 8th Rifle Brigade with 3RTR giving what assistance was possible. Strong artillery support with smokescreening off the flanks was promised.

I was to contact the CO of Northants Yeomanry and advise him of enemy strongpoints, in particular the enemy 88s out to the west. As they moved through our positions I ran over to the CO's tank and told him: 'For God's sake, don't go too far out to the west or you will come under 88 fire from Ifs!'

I pointed out where several of my burnt-out tanks were still smouldering and I presumed he would heed my warning. However, unaccountably, his tanks moved out to the west, trying to outflank the village. In a matter of moments about twenty of the regiment's tanks were hit, most of them bursting into flames. The remainder withdrew back through my position in some confusion.

Down by the embankment, Colonel David had seen this happen and gave orders that 3RTR would now support this attack. The artillery fire came down on the villages, smokescreens were also put down on both flanks giving excellent cover and we were able to advance more or less in line with the Rifle Brigade companies.

As I moved forward out of my shelter, with an almighty crash the tank shuddered and crunched to a halt. I bailed out with my operator and gunner, all unhurt, and inspected the tank. An 88mm shell had gone straight through the front of the tank, killing the driver and co-driver outright. I gave orders to my two crewmen to make their way back to the embankment and dashed over to my nearest tank, commanded by troop sergeant Freddie Dale. He very reluctantly got out and I took command of his tank. At last we were able to move properly and give good supporting fire to the infantry entering the village. There was still a lot of 88mm fire coming from the area of Ifs to the west so I took my three remaining tanks to the western edge of the village to prevent any penetration from that direction.

We had an excellent shoot at some fleeing Germans, also knocking out two more Panthers that attempted to come into the village from the west. B and C squadrons, also depleted and down to two or three tanks each, entered the village at the same time. We were able to knock down the walls of houses, from where cowering Germans emerged with their hands raised. Anti-tank guns were knocked out at point-blank range and in a matter of about an hour the village was cleared.

Some 300 panzer grenadiers were killed, wounded or taken prisoner during the attack, with over twenty anti-tank guns of various sizes accounted for. It was said later in a history of the division that this had been a model exhibition of an attack by armour and infantry.

At about 7 p.m., with H and F companies well settled in the village, Colonel David came forward with his RHQ and rallied the remaining 3RTR tanks on the western edge of Bras. We were holding an O group when a shell landed in the middle of the group and the recce troop officer, Maurice Thompson, was killed along with two other crew members.

We still had another task that evening. Our faithful G Company, Rifle Brigade was to attack the other village, Hubert-Folie, with a squadron of the Fife and Forfar Yeomanry in support, and 3RTR giving what support we could from Bras. This we were able to do and in a matter of about an hour the village was taken with no great loss on our side. Again, a number of prisoners were captured, along with several intact anti-tank guns with their crews.

And so ended Operation Goodwood for 3RTR. It had been a hard battle with two days of heavy fighting. The battalion had lost well over sixty tanks with heavy personnel losses. In my own squadron I had lost seventeen tanks out my complement of nineteen, over half being completely destroyed. All my officers were casualties, except Johnny Langdon, and only one troop sergeant, Buck Kite, was with me at the end. Practically every man in the squadron had bailed out at least once.

The battalion was pulled out for a rest and refitting and it says much for the resilience of the crews remaining that ten days later we were back up to strength in men and tanks and ready for the next operation.

During action there is no time for sentiment, no time to dwell on casualties or loss of crewmen one had known in battle, but later, during rest periods when letters home to wives and loved ones are being written, it is brought home very forcibly and the loss of old friends is felt more deeply.

Goodwood had been a difficult battle for 3RTR and even some of the old hands had felt the strain. During our few days of rest and reorganisation three fairly senior sergeants who had been with the regiment from the desert days formed up and requested permission to be released from tank duties. This was an unusual request from experienced troop sergeants, but there comes a time when a man's courage and fortitude can run out. This time, after a few days of comparative peace and quiet in the echelon lines, two of the three returned to duty and served in tanks until the end of the war.

A few days later we moved back across the River Orne and prepared for what we thought could be the break-out from the bridgehead: Operation Bluecoat.

Chapter Eighteen

Back to the Bocage: Operation Bluecoat

On 25 July General Bradley's First US Army launched its break-out in the west, from a start-line along the St Lo–Periers road. For the first forty-eight hours the advance was slow, but, faced by weaker and shallower defences than had opposed Goodwood, the break-through, when it came, was sudden and dramatic. General Patton's Third Army was quickly activated and that flamboyant and dynamic leader drove his army fast and deep through the German defences south to Avranches, before swinging east to trap most of the German Army in what would be called the Falaise Pocket in mid–August.

Following Goodwood, 11th Armoured Division had been pulled out of the line to lick its wounds, replace tanks and crews and move west to prepare for the next attack, Operation Bluecoat. Launched on 29 July, 11th Armoured was to advance south from Caumont, through the thick bocage country towards St Martin des Besaces, Le Beny Bocage and Vire. At the extreme western end of Second British Army, and liaising closely with the Americans on their right, 11th Armoured played an important part in containing the Germans within the ever-shrinking Falaise Pocket.

During our few days' rest and reorganisation it had been decided at higher levels that the grouping of the brigades within the division could also be reorganised. In the light of the result of Operation Goodwood, when the armour had operated without any weight of infantry in support, and the consequent losses of tanks attacked from villages that had not been cleared, it was decided that in future an infantry battalion would move with an armoured regiment – in fact, it would actually travel on the backs of the tanks – and that any armoured regiment must be prepared to work with any infantry battalion.

This change in the method of operations was implemented immediately and in our subsequent operations, right up to the Baltic, proved most successful.

On 29 July we moved across the congested rear of the Second Army with the rest of the 11th Armoured Division, back into the dreaded bocage countryside. We had learned at a CO's O group that we would be operating on the immediate flank of the Americans.

Our last objectives, the villages of Le Beny-Bocage and St Martin-des-Besaces, were both in deep bocage. My second captain, Neil Kent, who had been left out of the battle at Goodwood, had rejoined the squadron; Johnny Langdon was still commanding 1 Troop. I told Neil to take over 2 Troop, with Buck Kite and Freddie Dale as troop sergeants to retain command of 3 and 4 troops.

Our advance through the bocage was slow, all tank commanders being very wary of the presence of German infantry lying behind the high hedges and banks – ideal terrain for their bazooka men to ambush the tanks.

I received orders from Colonel David to move on to St Martin-des-Besaces. We had infantry from the Shropshires on the backs of our tanks. We moved part of the way on the first night. I had Neil Kent and Buck Kite's troops in the lead. It was a pitch-black night and they were to be congratulated on finding their way almost up to the railway line just to the north of the village. The two troops took up a position in an orchard beside a small farm. The infantry dug themselves into a cornfield in front of the orchard to await first light. Together with the remainder of the squadron, I was about half a mile away, with the rest of the Shropshires digging in around me.

At first light we stood to in our tanks. All seemed quiet and I gave orders for crews to brew up. I had called up Neil Kent to come and see me to discuss our move on to the village and he duly arrived as we were having breakfast. At about 9.30 a.m. we were all out of our tanks, when shot and shell came whistling all around us. Most of us scrambled into our tanks, with others taking shelter beneath them. I could also hear the sharp crack of tank fire from the direction of Buck Kite's troop. Shortly afterwards, Buck reported over the air that he was being attacked by several Panthers and his position was critical. Telling Neil to get back to his troop as quickly as possible I prepared to move with my other two troops to their assistance. It was then that we also came under fire from two Panther tanks that had crept up almost unseen. One of Freddie Dale's troop was hit almost immediately but his other tank with the seventeen-pounder retaliated by knocking out one of the Panthers and forcing the other to retire.

I reported to Colonel David that we were under attack from Panthers – so far an unspecified number of them. I was a little worried about the position of the infantry but after consultation with the Shropshire company commander, who seemed quite happy that he had several men ready with Piats should the Panthers pursue their attack, I felt a little more reassured.

Shortly afterwards, Peter Elstob, one of Buck Kite's corporal commanders, reported that Buck had been badly wounded, his tank was out of action and another tank in his troop was also completely destroyed.

Colonel David came on the air to tell me that a squadron of the Guards Brigade would be coming up on our left to support us on that flank. In the meantime, Neil Kent had rallied his troop with the remnants of Buck's troop and was making a determined attempt to cross the railway line into the village, but reported being held up by anti-tank fire from guns among the houses. I rallied my half of the squadron and quickly moved up to the line of the railway and we took up our positions there where we could support our infantry who were moving into the village. The Shropshires made good progress with our own mobile infantry, G Company, Rifle Brigade, giving excellent support and very soon the village was in our hands. We were able to cross the railway line and give good close support whilst they were clearing up the enemy pockets of resistance. One Panther tank was knocked out in the market place before the village was finally cleared.

When Colonel David came up with his RHQ he informed me that C Squadron had been successful in support of a battalion of the KSLI in capturing Le Beny-Bocage, so both villages were now in our hands.

There now followed a very unpleasant period of close fighting in an infantry role in this unsuitable tank country. It did, however, give us great experience in our co-operation with the infantry companies. Sometimes we would be working with the Shropshires, next day with the Herefords and so on, giving us the opportunity to get to know intimately the various company commanders. I am quite sure this experience contributed to a great extent towards the successes which came later.

One such example occurred as we were advancing towards Flers at Le Bar Perrier Ridge. A company of the Shropshire had dug themselves in on the ridge but were surrounded by enemy tanks. A squadron of the 23rd Hussars commanded by Len Hagger, a good friend of mine, had been sent forward to support them, but after about twenty-four hours of constant attacks from Panthers in his rear had lost about half of his squadron. At about 3 a.m. Colonel David gave me orders to take my squadron up to the ridge to relieve Hagger. It meant moving through an enemy-occupied village which was being heavily shelled by our artillery.

I gave orders to move out, Johnny Langdon's troop in front, my HQ tanks following and the remainder of the squadron at the rear. I told all commanders to go through the village at speed, orders which I think were unnecessary as practically all the houses were on fire and nobody would wish to hang about. We motored through at about 25mph, seeing no enemy, and proceeded up the hill towards Len Hagger's tanks, some of which we could see were burning.

I found the squadron commander trying to rally his tanks. He was pleased to see me and greeted me with the wry comment, 'You've come to a lovely spot, Bill. Hope you fare better than me!' He told me where to find the company commander of the infantry and left rather hurriedly to the rear, telling me as he left, 'Most of my tanks were knocked out from behind.' Not a very reassuring thought.

I went forward and reported to the infantry commander that I was in position and that we would stand to at first light. I gave orders to all the tank commanders to tuck their tanks in the hedgerows to get as much concealment as possible and we settled down to await dawn.

As the light came up we were ready in our tanks, rather apprehensive and expecting to be greeted by a hail of shot and shell. Nothing happened, all was quiet and after a while I gave orders to brew up. We were all out of our tanks, my own crews busily making breakfast, when, with one enormous crash, the turret of my tank disintegrated, showering us with metal. Apart from a few scratches no one was hurt, with the exception of the damage to my pride. I had given orders for all tanks to conceal themselves and here was my own tank disabled. It was the only enemy shot fired. Apparently they had pulled out from their positions in front of the Shropshires, leaving one last anti-tank gun to have a final crack at us.

Shortly afterwards, I received orders to return to the battalion area and somewhat sheepishly reported the loss of my tank to the CO.

A few days later we captured Flers. Not many enemy were in occupation and it was the first large town to fall into our hands. The tanks didn't stay in the town for very long but our infantry brigade were lucky enough to spend a few days in Flers celebrating with the delighted citizens.

After this unpleasant spell in the bocage, 3RTR were pleased to reach Laigle and be given five days' rest. We parked our tanks in a series of orchards around the town and proceeded to enjoy ourselves. We were able to have much-needed baths, wash our filthy clothes and generally indulge in self-decontamination. A cinema show was arranged by the local mayor and a dance was also organised in the town. The troops' exuberance was somewhat subdued and the dance was not quite the success it might have been as nearly all the local ladies were accompanied by either their mothers or French male friends.

My own enjoyment of these few days' rest was rather spoilt by a spell of illness which laid me low for the whole period. I developed a virus and rash which turned out to be a re-occurrence of malaria, something which had not happened since my days in Africa.

When we moved on, our objective was to advance to the Seine with part of our plan to help close the gap on Falaise. Canadians and the 1st Polish Armoured Division were closing in on the Germans from one side and the Americans from the other. The 11th Armoured Division was to hold the 'bottom of the bag'. The story of the Falaise Gap is well-known: 40,000 prisoners were taken and countless tanks, self-propelled guns and other armoured vehicles destroyed.

We had no time to linger; on 28 August we moved on and crossed the Seine at Vernon. It was to be the start of one of the most exciting and momentous advances by an armoured division in the Second World War: 386 miles in eight days, culminating in the capture of the port of Antwerp.

Chapter Nineteen

A Continental Tour: Amiens

The next task of the 11th Armoured Division was to advance with the utmost speed to Amiens, capture the bridges over the Somme and establish the division in that area.

At my CO's O group I had learned that 3RTR would lead the right-hand column of the division in this advance to the Somme. I also learned that my squadron would again be at the sharp end.

Eight o'clock on an overcast evening and the battalion was busily refuelling and replenishing ammunition. The men were weary and wanting to get their heads down. Permission had been given to make a brew and on my return to the squadron a mug of hot tea was pushed into my hands. My tank commanders were assembled, awaiting my return. 'Orders, sir?'

They were simple: 'Pack up and be ready to move in figures three zero. We are to drive on to Amiens at thirty minutes' notice. We are leading squadron.'

'Roll on, not again,' someone said.

'Your squadron will lead, Bill,' the CO had told me. 'Don't let anything stop you.'

By now it was raining hard. Amiens lay more than twenty miles away through enemy-held territory. There was no moonlight. I told my 1 Troop commander, 'Johnny, your troop will lead. Don't stop for anything.' My squadron was already at the head of the column in the village of Fontaine Bonnelieu. I would move the squadron with 1 Troop leading, my HQ tanks following and the rest of the squadron bringing up the rear. We would be closely followed by G Company, Rifle Brigade in half-tracks and lorries, then the other tanks of the battalion and the infantry.

Rain was streaming off the hulls of the Shermans as I walked down the line to make sure each tank commander knew what was expected of him About 10.30 p.m., in pitch black, the advance began. All preparations had been made; it was now up to the drivers.

Huddled in their turrets, the commanders studied their maps by shaded light, headphones humming and water trickling down their necks. Operators tinkered with the radios, and the 75mm gunners, having checked and re-checked their ammunition stocks, hunched in their seats, damp and weary behind their useless sights. They could afford to relax slightly. For the drivers, however, there was no relief. In front of the first Sherman, Johnny Langdon's tank, stretched an unfamiliar road, some-times reflecting the pale sheen of distant searchlights. Hatch open and head out, the driver could only stare into the darkness and obey instruc-tions. The head poking out of the hatch on the other side of the hull belonged to the co-driver, who was manning the .30 machine gun. If there was trouble, they would be the first to suffer.

For the drivers following it was a question of maintaining the required distance and keeping their eyes on the dark shape in front. Unlike the circus elephants, we had no tails to hold. Nevertheless, the circus was going to town.

A mile passed without incident. And another. The headphones' drowsy hum was broken by a crackle. The message from the CO was, 'Push on – push on!' A line of hills appeared, silhouetted in the soft blue glow of the far-off searchlights still sweeping the sky. 'Keep going, Sugar One. Press on.' The driver of Sugar One, the leading tank, with steering sticks in his hands, maintained speed.

Things began to happen at the first (and only) cross-roads between our start point and the outskirts of Amiens. Sugar One reported a column of horse-drawn artillery and limbers on the road, too close to engage with his guns.

'Okay, Sugar One. Motor through them. Run over anything that gets in your way. Out.' Soon we came across splintered wreckage and writhing mounds. Vague shapes were stampeding over the fields.

'Keep going. Press on.' The words came monotonously from the CO to me, to Sugar One, to the drivers with chilled faces and strained eyes. 'Keep going!'

Two miles further on, with visibility down to twenty feet, a Volkswagen appeared directly in front of the lead tank. Johnny, with my constant urgings ringing in his ears, ordered his driver to speed up and overtake it. The little car skidded wildly and was crushed. Though the passenger was killed, the driver managed to clamber out and as the Sherman manoeuvred free of the wreckage, began to stammer and shout. When it dawned on him that it was no panzer that had hit him, he burst into hysterical laughter and stumbled down the column. The sound of automatic fire came faintly through the night as engines revved again.

More humming – more crackling. Sugar One was having quite a night. A large object was parked across our route, half blocking it. 'Sugar One – am engaging enemy tank on the road in front of me – Sugar One out!' The column slowed. In every turret there was a spark of interest, gunners shifting their positions, radio operators twiddling their knobs afresh.

From my turret I saw in quick succession three flashes send shadows racing across the dripping fields. Inky darkness closed over us again, only to be dispelled by a ball of orange and yellow flames which scattered burning fragments over a wide area. Heavy concussion indicated the enemy tank was carrying a full load of ammunition. Sugar Two had fired three rounds of solid shot from a range of twenty feet and quickly reversed. Three men, who had probably been asleep, scrambled out of the wreck and ran a few yards before it blew up. It was quite the biggest and best explosion we had seen for some time.

About three miles from Amiens we pulled off the road. I realised we had rather left the rest of the column behind except for G Company. I had a quick chat with Noel Bell and we decided we would wait for the rest to catch up with us. I even gave permission for a quick brew but the first mugs of tea had barely been gulped down when we were ordered to make all speed. I put another troop in the lead to give Sugar One a break.

What they say about the cold light of dawn is true: it does help to concentrate your thoughts. Though the appearance of German transport going about its normal business implied the enemy was still unaware of our presence, I felt this incredible state of affairs wouldn't last.

We engaged target after target. The countryside was littered with burning wrecks, alive with running figures. Somewhere the alarm bells must be ringing; maybe the night trek was to prove the easy bit. I did not believe this – my previous experience said, 'No, nothing's easy.' The idea of plunging into an unknown town didn't appeal to me at all. I remembered Calais too well. Of Amiens I knew only that it had given its name to a big battle in which the Tank Corps played a leading part in the Great War. We had already passed one or two British military cemeteries.

After four years of occupation, during which its goods yard and surrounding rail network had been regularly bombed, the city was run down. Clattering over the uneven paves, past patches of waste ground, rows of dingy houses and dilapidated factories, I thought, 'What a place to die for!' The driver and co-driver had already closed their hatches and I sank further into the turret. Too many tank commanders had been shot in the head.

Some armed men standing on a corner signalled us to stop. A number of Brownings swung in their direction. They turned out to be the Resistance fighters from a well-organised Maquis. I asked them anxiously about the best way to 'Le Pont'. They said they could show me but did I know there were about 4,000 enemy troops in the city, some of them with anti-tank guns?

At this stage my squadron consisted of ten tanks. Noel Bell, who came up to confer, told me rather plaintively that his company strength was seventy riflemen. Nevertheless we decided that as the rest of 3RTR and the Rifle Brigade were coming up we would push on, the lead tanks being covered by the others. Road blocks are useless unless they are substantial and well defended. The enemy had been given no time to organise themselves and at the first barricade all eyes looked for the opposition.

Bang! The enemy gunner must have been nervous. His shot demolished a hardware shop and before another could be fired, the position had been smothered in .5 Browning fire. An abandoned lorry and a couple of carts were swept aside by a Sherman and we moved on. Impressed by this success, excited maquisards climbed onto the back of the tanks and pointed out the way forward and the known enemy positions.

The buildings got taller and the back of my neck grew pricklier but gradually, shooting now and then, we made our way to the river. And there it was – a large bridge, deserted. I scanned the houses on the distant

140

bank through binoculars but saw little sign of activity. The people of Amiens were sensibly lying low. So was the enemy.

I ordered Sugar Three to cross the bridge and the first Sherman moved over in quick time, reported no opposition and was promptly reinforced by the rest of the troop. I prepared to join them. My driver advanced – we emerged from the shelter of a side street, increased speed and were climbing the approach road when, only a few yards away, the bridge was enveloped in smoke and collapsed noisily into the river. Reversing hurriedly into cover we waited for the dust to clear. I quickly told my troop commander on the other side to take up an observation position and saw their exhaust smoke vanish among the silent houses. It was just after 7 a.m.

I was somewhat concerned about my troop on the other side of the river but one of the excited maquisards on my tank said that only about 800 yards away there was another bridge, not mined and being guarded by some of his section. We could cross there. I told my isolated troop commander, Bill Yates, the situation and said I hoped the rest of the squadron would be with him shortly.

He was rather excited, reporting that just around the corner from his position were four 88mm anti-tank guns already limbered up with their half-tracks, ready to move off. I told him not to get too involved, but, if he could, to prevent them escaping. I promised support as soon as possible. In the event he sealed off both ends of the road and captured all four guns with their crews. Later on he was awarded the Military Cross for his conduct in this episode.

I then moved the rest of the squadron to the other bridge that was held by the Maquis. We crossed over and by this time our infantry had taken over the bridge without any problems. The entire division eventually used this bridge to cross the Somme. Joining up with Bill Yates' troop I found him guarding the 88mm guns and about fifty rather disconsolate Germans sitting on the roadside. It was a fitting end to our drive on Amiens.

Chapter Twenty

On to Antwerp

Following our success in the capture of Amiens, there was a certain amount of justifiable euphoria in 3RTR and this was further amplified by a letter of congratulations from the army commander to General Roberts, which was then passed on to the leading units.

We were not allowed to linger in Amiens or to rest on our laurels, for the next day, 1 September, we learned that we were to push on with all speed – possible objective, Brussels. We were on the left of the divisional centre-line with B Squadron leading. My squadron was in reserve so a fairly uneventful day was anticipated. We were able to cover about fifty miles the first day with very little opposition. We spent a rather uncomfortable night halted by the roadside, during the course of which we came under some artillery shelling, which forced us to get into our tanks. There were also one or two scares about panzerfaust parties attacking the 23rd Hussars on our right.

The next day we continued the advance, C Squadron leading with Johnny Dunlop in command. At about 2 p.m. we were halted some five miles south-west of Lille, which we understood was still held by the Germans. No orders were given for us to attack the town and we wondered why. We sat around for the rest of the day and again spent a rather unpleasant night on the roadside. However, we then learned the reason: our objective was not to be Brussels but the port of Antwerp.

We had something of a problem because our intelligence officer couldn't find enough maps to go round and those he had were very small scale. We had orders to move very early on 3 September and when I reported to Colonel David's tank for orders, I was told that A Squadron would be leading the advance. There was a little excitement early on when the battalion signals officer, investigating a small wood, emerged with fifty prisoners and their company payroll! They seemed quite happy to surrender.

We moved on, Johnny Langdon's 1 Troop in the lead; our objective, Antwerp, lay some ninety miles ahead and in spite of instructions to move at all speed, I had briefed my tank commanders to be watchful for panzer-faust ambushes. Their particular ploy was to lie still in the ditches beside the road, let the leading tanks pass, then stand up and let fly into the side of the nearest tank.

We moved on without any trouble until we were about a mile short of the town of Seclin, which lay directly in our path. I was not sure if the town was occupied but as I had two of the recce troop's Honeys with my leading troop, I gave orders for them to investigate. They had only advanced about 100 yards when with an almighty crash both Honeys careered off the road in flames. By the sound of the explosion, we knew that 88s were about.

I gave orders for the squadron to take cover while I assessed the position. Looking through my binoculars at the woods and orchards around the town, I thought I could make out several gun positions in both areas. I reported to the CO that I thought the town was well occupied and protected by anti-tank guns. Colonel David's solution was that A Squadron would race across the open fields which led up to the town at speed to draw the enemy's fire while B Squadron would then close in and engage the enemy positions thus revealed.

Needless to say, when I briefed my troop commanders with the plan it was not received with any great enthusiasm. I gave orders to move more or less in line and we set off for the outskirts of the town. There was a bit of dead ground just short of the orchards and I hoped we would make that without too many casualties. I think the enemy gunners were rather surprised to see so many Shermans approaching at speed and their firing was rather haphazard: although AP shot was whistling around us we managed to get to cover in the dead ground.

Neil Kent, my second-in-command, reported that his tank was hit but not penetrated and only one other tank had been hit. We were able to take up good hull-down positions and give excellent supporting fire to B Squadron as they entered the town.

I gave orders for the squadron to advance and 1 Troop moved quickly into the centre of the town, knocking out an anti-tank gun with its crew en route. I moved into the town with the remainder of the squadron without any further problems. B Squadron had knocked out several anti-tank guns, overrunning a complete battery, and it dispersed a desperately fleeing transport echelon trying to escape from the town. By midday the town was in our hands.

In the meantime Johnny Langdon reported quietly to me that one of his tank commanders had found a huge shed stacked with crates and boxes marked 'Werhmacht only'. They were full of bottles of champagne, brandy, wine and liqueurs. I gave instructions to all my tank commanders to discreetly draw their tanks up to the shed; when the advance resumed, most of the squadron's tanks had crates of brandy and champagne hidden under the bedrolls behind their turrets.

About this time we heard the noise of battle from our right flank. The 23rd Hussars were being heavily engaged: some tanks and artillery fire were giving them a hard time. One Tiger tank appeared and knocked out several of our soft-skinned vehicles, but was engaged by our twenty-five-pounders at close range and driven off. Although this action held up the drivers by about two hours, 23rd Hussars reported that they had crossed the border and at 2 p.m. were at Tournai. By about 3.30 p.m. 3RTR, with A Squadron in the lead, had reached the frontier at Willems.

A rather enthusiastic subaltern came on the air and said, 'Doesn't anyone realise we are now in Belgium?' As we were rather proud of our wireless discipline, everyone was most interested in the CO's response, which was colourful to say the least.

Following winding lanes that led to the Escaut Canal, we sent a recce party ahead to see if the bridge was still intact. A sergeant reported that it had still not been repaired after it had been blown in 1940. Near Warcoing, Bill Yates, my 2 Troop leader, who was doing a recce down the canal, found a wooden bridge that was undamaged. On inspection, I wondered if the bridge would stand up to a column of Shermans. I called up a Honey from the recce troop, deciding to test it with the lighter tank. There was no problem, so a Sherman then trundled slowly across. The bridge creaked a bit but held and the rest went over one by one.

144

It was with some relief that the CO ordered us to go on to Renaix. It had begun to rain hard, making things rather difficult and miserable, but the town was unoccupied and the population went mad with joy. We didn't stop but pushed on towards Odenarde.

My squadron had been relieved of the lead and Johnny Dunlop's C Squadron took over. It was always a nice feeling to be in reserve, to be able to relax a little. Point tank, point troop or point squadron was not a position to be envied in these latter stages of the campaign.

The battalion halted near Zottegem to refuel. Whilst halted, one of C Squadron's Shermans was hit by an 88mm anti-tank gun, which was very quickly dealt with by the other tanks. There was a quick flurry of action from some panzerfaust men, but the Shermans hosed the hedges and ditches with their machine guns, eventually forcing several German soldiers to come out of the shadows with their hands up. They were huddled together, a miserable-looking group in the driving rain, until guards from our infantry were found.

At about 3 a.m. we leaguered just east of the town of Alost. We were all extremely wet and cold and most of us didn't even bother to put up our tarpaulin shelters but slept in or under our tanks. Quartermaster Paddy Hehir came up with the rations. I was always particularly pleased to see Paddy. We had been sergeants together before the war when the battalion was stationed at Warminster. He usually managed to bring me clean clothes and sometimes a bottle of whisky. It was with some dismay that we learned that Brigade HQ had heard of our windfall of liquid refreshment and he had orders to relieve us of it. In the end, nearly everyone managed to squirrel away a selection in blankets on the tank and Paddy finished up with all the less-favoured white wine. Brigade HQ had promised that it would all be distributed later, but that was the last we saw of it.

At about 5.30 a.m. next morning at the CO's tank we learned we were to advance on the city of Antwerp. The 23rd Hussars would be on our right and 3RTR was to try to gain entry into the city straight up the main road via Boom. Johnny Dunlop's C Squadron would lead, with my squadron in close support. B Squadron with its commander, Jock Balharrie, was to be in reserve, but also try and find another way into the city across the canals that surround the southern aspect.

We made good progress to Boom but Johnny Dunlop found the main bridge was mined. Fortunately a civilian named Vekemans, a Belgian engineer and a member of the Resistance, showed the squadron commander a smaller bridge across the canal which was clear, he himself having removed the mines just prior to our arrival. I learned later that he was awarded the Military Cross for his exploits.

The whole of the battalion was able to cross the bridge and gain entry into the city but not without some excitement. Small-arms fire came from some pillboxes on the other side of the river and I learned later that Jock Balharrie was badly wounded whilst crossing the bridge.

I was given instructions to branch off to the left of C Squadron and to make for the main railway station. Johnny Dunlop's squadron, with G Company, Rifle Brigade, was to make all haste to reach the docks.

The city was in turmoil. German horse artillery columns were milling about and being shot up by the Shermans' machine guns, and prisoners were being rounded up. The Belgian population surged onto the streets and it became almost impossible to advance. Every tank was greeted by cheering crowds who clambered up on to the turrets. Crews were over-whelmed with flowers, bottles and kisses. At some stage during this early euphoria one of the civilians on my tank, a man in a rather dirty old mac with a Sten gun looped over his shoulder, said he was a member of the Resistance and could show me a route to the station. Trying to get my squadron together among the crowds surrounding them was going to be difficult but over the air I told them to try and follow my tank. Colonel Silvertop was also having great difficulty in moving the battalion and his oft-repeated 'Push on' was having little effect. However, then some small-arms fire from a block of flats dispersed most of the civilians from the streets and we were able to move.

My friendly civilian gave his name as Gaston de Lausney. He spoke perfect English and I gathered he was a teacher. I told him to stick around and with his guidance managed to rally most of my tanks through several side streets and on to the station. As we approached the station buildings we came under fire both from small arms and at least one anti-tank gun.

146

I had a company of the 1st Herefords with me; at least I thought I had, but conversing with their company commander he informed me that he could only muster about thirty riflemen, most of the others had disappeared among the ecstatic civilians. By this time we were completely isolated from the remainder of the battalion, but from information coming over the air I gathered that C Squadron had reached the docks, having cleared up enemy pockets of resistance on the way. The docks were completely undamaged and the squadron, with G Company's assistance, spent the rest of the day dealing with small enemy groups and ensuring that the dock installations were not sabotaged.

Battalion HQ with B Squadron and the 4th KSLI, with Brigadier Churcher personally in command, cleared Central Park, where most of the Germans were concentrated. After a fierce battle the enemy garrison surrendered. General Von Stolberg and some 6,000 German soldiers were taken prisoner.

I was kept active trying to clear the railway station but it was beginning to get more and more difficult to bring the tanks into action as the civilians were once again crowding onto the streets. I had drawn my tank up close to a cafe opposite the station entrance and was able to engage at point-blank range a group of enemy infantry round an anti-tank gun. My gunner knocked out the gun and a section of the Herefords rounded up some forty Germans, who I am sure were rather relieved to be out of it.

There was still a number of enemy soldiers about. One of the civilians in the cafe told me that just round the corner from the station a German HQ was located in a large private house. He suggested that a couple of shots from the 'beeg cannon' – meaning the seventeen-pounder – would easily deal with the matter. Two rounds were duly fired, which knocked out the windows in the house and a rather bewildered German staff stumbled out and gave itself up to the tank commander. The window of the cafe also collapsed to the delight of the crowd inside. The empty shell cases were then put on display in the window casing. (Some years later, on a visit to Antwerp, I managed to find the cafe – the shell cases were still proudly displayed in the window.)

My task was not over, although practically all resistance in the city had ended. I was told to rally my squadron in the station area and to remain there. RHQ, with the other two squadrons, were withdrawn to a large chateau on the outskirts of the city. The Belgian civilians were now breaking open bottle after bottle of champagne and a somewhat riotous party developed. I remained in constant touch with the adjutant over the air and suggested that it might be a good idea if we could be withdrawn. I was a little worried that things might get out of hand. The company commander of the Herefords was also concerned about his missing company. It was not until about first light that I received orders to withdraw and join the battalion in the chateau grounds.

It had been an incredible day, practically all the city was in our hands. One small disappointment was the fact that the main bridge over the canal in Antwerp was blown after we had taken over the city. This put the suburb of Merxem out of bounds and the enemy made full use of this mistake. (General Roberts, in his book, *From the Desert to the Baltic*, suggests that this omission to capture the bridge when the division first entered the city was probably the worst mistake he had made during the entire campaign.)

The next few days were spent in servicing our tanks, refitting and receiving reinforcements after out hectic advance from Normandy to Antwerp; 386 miles in eight days was a quite remarkable achievement. This epic advance by an armoured division was unparalleled in the Second World War. The journey was never easy, with determined German rearguard actions encountered every step of the way. This operation had also taken its toll on some of the tank crews, including my own. Ever since we had our few days' rest at Laigle, I had been suffering from a virus of some sort and it was only after I was seen by the divisional medics that I was told I had malaria. However, the attack was more serious than I thought and, in spite of my protests, I was ordered home on the next plane.

On landing in the UK I was immediately hospitalised in Netley Hospital for a thorough check-up. Three or four days later I was transferred to the Cambridge Military Hospital at Aldershot, where I spent the next three weeks. After my discharge from hospital I managed to get a few days' leave before joining 152 RAC, a rehabilitation unit stationed near Newmarket. During my stay there I received the news that I had been awarded a bar to the Military Cross for my efforts in the capture of Amiens and the bridge over the Somme. I spent Christmas at my parents' home in Uppingham, together with my wife who also joined us there on leave from the ATS.

In early February I received orders to report back to 3RTR, which was enjoying a well-earned rest at Poperinghe following its successful efforts in the Ardennes battle where it knocked out a number of tanks of the 2nd Panzer Division at Dinant. In effect, this action extinguished Hitler's last hopes for success in the Ardennes.

The battalion had just taken over the new British tank, the Comet, and was engaged in full preparation for the Rhine crossing. I had hoped to take over my old A Squadron, but the new CO, Lieutenant Colonel Teddy Mitford, decided that Neil Kent, my previous second-in-command, should retain command on his promotion to major. B Squadron, however, was available and I was quite happy to take over a new command. My second-in-command was Captain Freddie Dingwell, who I knew very well, with troop commanders Wadsworth, Rylands, Ricketts and Montgomery, all of whom had been with the battalion since D-Day.

Quite a lot had happened during my absence from 3RTR. Colonel David Silvertop had been killed in quite tragic circumstances when the battalion had not even been in close combat. A group of senior officers, including Brigadier Roscoe Harvey, the brigade commander, and Colonel Silvertop were having an O group by the side of the road when two German half-tracks came out of a farmyard nearby, spraying the group with bullets. Colonel David, Lieutenant Colonel Orr, CO of the Monmouths, and a corporal were killed instantly whilst Brigadier Roscoe was slightly wounded. It was of no consolation that the half-tracks were summarily dealt with immediately. Lieutenant Colonel Teddy Mitford, who I knew very well, had then arrived to take over the battalion.

Chapter Twenty-One

The Drive to the Baltic

I was fortunate enough to have a few days in Poperinghe to familiarise myself with my new squadron. I knew most of the troop commanders and several of the more senior NCOs, but during my absence the battalion had been engaged in actions in Holland and the Ardennes. Some casualties had been sustained and replacement crew members had been necessary.

We were also all involved in getting to know our new tank, the Comet. We found it to be an excellent tank. It was better armed than the Sherman, and had a much lower profile; it was very fast and manoeuvrable and the 77mm gun was an extremely efficient weapon. We had hoped that the Comet would be armed with the seventeen-pounder, as on the Sherman Firefly, but it had not been possible to fit it in the turret. We consoled ourselves with the thought that perhaps at this stage in the war we might not meet many Tiger or Panther tanks. We also felt that perhaps the Ardennes battle would be the last major clash of armour and from now on it would be a matter of dealing with German rearguard actions – from experience, an operation they were extremely good at.

Shortly before leaving Poperinghe, at the CO's O group we learned that 11th Armoured Division would not be with us in the initial assault across the Rhine but, in conjunction with the 6th Airborne Division, would be involved in the dash to the Elbe. Accordingly we moved up to the Rhine at Wesel, crossing the river by the long Bailey bridge without any difficulties. Wesel was completely destroyed, having been subjected to heavy bombardment by both sides, and the town was just a pile of rubble.

Our first objective was the town of Burgsteinfurt. 3RTR, with the infantry of the 1st Herefords on the backs of the tanks, moved up to the town, which was found to be fairly heavily defended. A Squadron in the lead had a couple of tanks knocked out and it was decided that the

Infantry Brigade would mount a major attack at night. This proved difficult but, after some heavy fighting, the town was taken by the infantry
battalion of 4KSLI and 1 Herefords, supported by B and C squadrons of
3RTR. During the street fighting three tanks of C Squadron were
knocked out, whilst two of my squadron were also brewed up by panzer-
faust attacks.

The next morning we moved on, with A Squadron in the lead, but the
advance was held up by a small river; this was quickly bridged by
the Royal Engineers, whilst being protected by a company of the Rifle
Brigade. We were ordered to leaguer for the night, most of the tanks by
the side of the road. What with all the bridging vehicles and general traffic
taking part in the night operations, not much sleep was possible.

At Colonel Mitford's O group that night we were warned that the
advance would continue at first light, C Squadron leading, with 3RTR's
next objective being the River Ems at Emsdetten. The leading squadron
reached the Ems at about 7.30 a.m. but found the bridge there destroyed,
so the squadron commander was told to push on down to Mesum where
it was hoped to find a bridge intact. However, there was no bridge at
Mesum either but the sapper major travelling with the leading squadron
considered the site to be a better bridging possibility than at Emsdetten
and called up his bridging party. They were soon under way, with a
company of 8th Rifle Brigade giving protection. The farther bank of the
river appeared to be undefended and a company of the KSLI was very
soon across and proceeded to secure the area completely. With no inter-
ference, the bridging party was able to complete the bridge by about
6 p.m. and 3RTR prepared to cross, with my squadron taking the lead.

My leading troop, 2 Troop with Lieutenant Frank Wadsworth in
command, moved on rapidly and reached the Dortmund–Ems Canal in
about an hour and a half with no problems en route. I closed up with the
rest of the squadron. Wadsworth had reported over the air that both
bridges were destroyed and that there was some enemy activity on the
other side of the canal. This area was known as the Teutenberger Wald;
it was heavily wooded with precipitous slopes and it obviously provided
an extremely good defensive position, which the enemy was quite
prepared to exploit.

As I moved in close behind 2 Troop we came under heavy artillery fire and extensive machine-gun fire from the dense woods. This was no great problem for the tanks but it was obviously going to be a difficult proposition to get bridging parties in action. I reported the situation to the CO and was told to tuck ourselves away into some sort of cover and not to get involved, orders with which I was quite happy to comply. At an O group that evening attended by both Brigadier Roscoe Harvey and Brigadier Jack Churcher, it was decided a squadron of 3RTR would be ferried across the canal that night by means of a ferry that the retreating enemy had left intact.

I was rather relieved that C Squadron was chosen for this particular operation. However, with Jock Balharrie commanding and in conjunction with a company of the KSLI, they crossed over without any great problems and established themselves in a small but secure bridgehead on the other side. In trying to then push forwards through the woods, C Squadron lost two tanks from anti-tank fire and it became clear that the enemy was in some strength in the woods and on top of the escarpment.

Later that evening the bridge across the canal was completed and early next morning the remainder of 3RTR joined C Squadron in the rather congested area. Several efforts were made to enlarge the bridgehead but even with the assistance of the 2nd Fife and Forfar Yeomanry, who had joined us in the bridgehead, little progress was made that day. In one abortive attack, the yeomanry, with 1st Herefords supported by the divisional artillery, was still not able to break through the enemy strongpoint. Some satisfaction was gained by the knocking out and capture of some fifteen anti-tank guns and their crews.

There followed two or three days' heavy fighting in the difficult wooded terrain, with the enemy slowly giving way and retreating behind their rearguard parties. At this stage 3RTR was brought into reserve, and the 2nd Fife and Forfar Yeomanry took up the advance with the 3 Mons Regiment, but a few days later the 3 Monmouths was withdrawn from the division and took no further part in the campaign. It was a sad moment as the regiment had been with the division from its inception, involved in all the heavy fighting since D-Day, and it had sustained heavy casualties.

Our few days' rest was a great boost to our resolve. We were able to obtain baths and a change of clothing, always a bonus to morale. When we again took up the advance in the van of the division I think most of us were in a better frame of mind and more optimistic about the outcome. It had been noticeable up to this point that there had been a slight lack of 'get up and go' and individual commanders of the leading tanks were reluctant to 'go round the next corner'. Point troop or point tank was an unenviable position and it had become most important for squadron commanders to rotate strictly their leading troop, and for the troop commander to rotate his lead tank.

Our next objective was Osnabruck, with my squadron to lead, and, as at Amiens, another night march was involved. As I briefed my tank commanders I once again emphasised the need to watch out for panzer-faust parties.

The journey was not easy and the Germans' resistance was determined. We encountered several defended road blocks which had to be cleared under fire by the leading tanks, assisted in some cases by one of the tanks fitted with a steel bulldozer blade. The radio call sign for the bulldozer, 'George George' was in constant use that night. However, with no losses, the leading troop moved on to the river at Eversheide and the troop commander, Frank Wadsworth, reported in his typical way: 'I'm at the bridge and can see the bloody thing is mined. I can see what look like two fifty-pound bombs strapped to the side.'

As I moved up to the river and got close to the bridge I could confirm his report and see the bombs myself. Whilst I was reporting the situation to the CO, Wadsworth got out of his tank and although there was considerable enemy fire from across the river, clambered onto the bridge and managed to cut the connecting wires to the explosives. It was an extremely brave action as I had fully expected the bridge to be blown at any moment. His troop quickly crossed the bridge, followed closely by myself and the rest of the squadron, where we took up positions protecting the crossing. The capture of the bridge proved invaluable, since the whole division were able to use this crossing to continue the advance. Lieutenant Wadsworth very deservedly received the Military Cross for his efforts.

The next objective for the division was the crossing of the River Weser. The 29th Armoured Brigade, with 23rd Hussars in the lead, were on one route, with 159th Infantry Brigade in parallel on the other. Both made excellent progress and the line of the river was reached, where, as expected, all bridges were down. Bridging parties at Stolzenau and Schlusselburg were quickly put into operation, and 8th Rifle Brigade managed to get across the river and formed a strong bridgehead, despite determined German harassing tactics.

It was decided that this would be the major crossing point for the division but before the engineers could complete the bridges, strong enemy air attacks, carried out by JU88s and some Stukas, delayed the operations. Fighter cover was requested and, although the enemy persisted in their attacks, they were eventually driven off and the bridges completed early the next day, 7 April.

We then enjoyed one or two fairly easy days, moving on steadily with little or no opposition, squadrons alternating in the lead, and finally crossed the river at Neustadt and moved on to Schwarmstedt.

On 11 April 3RTR moved on from Schwarmstedt with my squadron in the lead. My leading troop commander was Second Lieutenant John Pearson, who had only recently joined the battalion, aged nineteen and with little battle experience. He had a very experienced troop sergeant with him, Sergeant Cranston, and another fairly new subaltern, Jeff Lomas, acting as his troop corporal. This was fairly common practice in RTR and was done specifically for young officers to gain battle experience. Our approach to the River Aller was via the village of Essel and I gave instructions to Pearson to keep a sharp look-out for possible panzerfaust men. In the event he reported only seeing a few dead Germans and he moved on rapidly towards the river. It was difficult tank country, a straight road leading across the river, the ground on either side of the road very marshy, making it impossible to deploy off the road.

I had moved my HQ tanks fairly close to Pearson's troop and, taking cover in a small stand of trees by the roadside, took stock of the position. Through my binoculars I thought I could see enemy movement in the woods across the river and accordingly warned Pearson to watch out and be prepared to engage anything that moved. 'Wilco, out,' was his response and he moved on towards the bridge. When, about 100 yards short of it, he could see that it was blown, he duly reported that fact to me and that he thought the river was about forty yards wide at that point.

I was somewhat concerned about the movement on the other side of the river as I knew that 1st Commando Brigade had made an assault crossing over the river the night before and we were not quite sure of their whereabouts. I was in the process of reporting to the CO that the bridge over the river was blown when suddenly – Crash! Bang! – Pearson's and Cranston's tanks erupted into flames and I could see one or two crew members out but obviously wounded. Lieutenant Lomas in the third tank managed to get off the road, took cover in some bushes, and proceeded to engage the anti-tank gun that had knocked out Pearson and Cranston. Although his tank was hit twice he courageously carried on the engagement and, eventually, with a direct hit on the enemy gun, knocked it out. In the meantime I moved up close to the burning tanks and got out to go to the aid of the wounded crews.

John Pearson and two of his crew, Shipley and Wyatt, his operator, were lying in the long grass beside the road, all badly burnt about the hands and face. Trooper Rowe, another member of his crew, had also managed to get clear and was not badly hurt. The driver Manning was killed instantly. Sergeant Cranston and Lieutenant Corporal Turnbull in the other tank were killed instantly, with the remainder of the crew managing to get out with only minor wounds.

There was some small-arms fire coming from across the river but not accurately enough to cause any problems and we were mostly concealed from view by the burning tanks. I immediately got on my radio for medical help and was told that Doc Whitehouse was on his way. Johnny Pearson's first few days with the battalion had been quite eventful, with two sharp engagements. In spite of his very serious burns, however, he was quite cheerful and without doubt was extremely thankful to be alive. He had also made every attempt to go to the aid of Cranston's crew. Shortly afterwards Doc Whitehouse arrived with his two medical half-tracks and the wounded were evacuated.

Orders came over the air from the CO that A Squadron was to be ferried across the river on rafts with a company of the KSLI. I was to give what cover fire I could with the remainder of my tanks and accordingly

155

to move up as close to the river line as possible. One of my old troop commanders in A Squadron, Johnny Langdon, was the leading troop across and he quickly moved his tanks up the tracks leading from the river with the infantry of KSLI moving through the woods on either side, on foot. Quite a number of enemy were flushed out of their foxholes in short, sharp skirmishes by the tanks and infantry, the KSLI sustaining some casualties in the process.

Some time later, as the situation appeared to be much quieter, Johnny gave permission for his crews to have a tea break. Suddenly there was armour-piercing shot whistling through the trees and one of his tanks was hit and disabled, the crew managing to bail out unhurt. A second shot tore through the turret, completely demolishing it. A Tiger tank had appeared only about a hundred yards away and proceeded to fire at everything in sight, particularly vehicles on the road. A scout car and another soft vehicle were soon ablaze.

It was obviously going to be a problem to make further advances along the road and it was not known if other panzers were roaming the woods; it was not normal for one tank to be operating on its own. Fortunately, some of C Squadron's tanks had managed to find a way round on the right flank through the woods in the rear of the Tiger. After a few anxious moments a rather excited voice over the radio said, 'I've got the bastard in my sights, here goes!' Sergeant Harding, one of C Squadron's troop sergeants, moved up to within a hundred yards of the enemy tank and with two well-placed AP shots brewed it up immediately.

Although there didn't appear to be any more panzers in the area, there was still a considerable number of enemy soldiers, mostly infantry, in well-dug-in positions, along with some anti-tank gun support. A Squadron, trying to push forward, lost another tank, with Lieutenant Bullock and Trooper Bligh, his driver, killed.

Johnny Langdon had orders to take his troop, now down to three tanks, in support of the infantry who were advancing through the woods. However, in trying to cross a small stream, two of his tanks became bellied down and his own tank became rather isolated. There was considerable mortar and Spandau fire coming down and his situation became rather serious. Fortunately orders came for him to withdraw to the line of the river. On his way back he was amazed to find that most of A Squadron was bogged down in the marshy ground – a most unpleasant situation – their tanks were unable to move, though still able to man their guns, hoping that another Tiger would not appear as they were sitting targets. Luckily nothing happened and although they spent a very wet and miserable night, all the tanks were recovered next morning by our own Royal Electrical Mechanical Engineers (REME) Light Aid detachment, commanded by Captain Charles Adkins.

That evening 3RTR leaguered near the village of Engehausen. Hot meals were organised, clothes dried and a welcome rum issue made us all feel almost human again. When we moved on next morning my squadron was in the lead. We were advancing through thickly wooded country and as progress was rather slow the infantry, a company of the 1st Herefords, decided to accompany the tanks on foot.

My leading troop – 1 Troop, with Lieutenant Don Ricketts in command – made good progress in the circumstances, encountering only sporadic small-arms fire from small groups of enemy infantry, which were soon dealt with. On reaching the small village of Winson, we found it unoccupied and I ordered Ricketts to push on towards Belsen. The name meant nothing to me and we could not have envisaged the horrors that were to come.

As we approached what obviously looked like a prison camp, a German vehicle suddenly appeared with two officers on board bearing a white flag. After some consultation with the infantry company commander, the two German officers were escorted back to Brigadier Churcher and thence to General Roberts, the divisional commander. From the information I gathered from the infantry commander, I understood that most of the inmates of the camp, many thousands, were seriously ill, and many were dead. Shortly afterwards, on instructions from Brigade HQ, we were told the camp was declared a 'no go' area. It was considered by both the Germans and ourselves that it would be highly dangerous if fighting continued in and around the camp, with the risk of the camp being broken open and the inmates allowed to roam the countryside spreading disease. The Germans were prepared to withdraw from the area. A time and withdrawal line was agreed and a special medical team was organised to investigate the camp.

In the meantime I and one or two of my tank commanders ventured into the camp to have a look around. I was not prepared for the horrific sights, even within the first few hundred yards of the camp entrance. The huts were full of almost-naked inmates, some dead, some only just alive and pitifully thin. There were bodies everywhere – lying in the small ditches around the huts; the stench was indescribable. As we understood the camp extended a possible mile or two further back it was impossible to imagine what the conditions would be like there. It was something I shall never forget and I beat a hasty retreat back to my squadron.

By this time the CO had brought up the remainder of the battalion and we went into leaguer a few hundred yards outside the camp to await further orders. This mini-halt continued until 10 a.m. the next day and when the advance continued 3RTR and 4KSLI were directed on to Luneberg and the River Elbe.

Luneberg was taken with practically no opposition and C Squadron, the leading squadron of 3RTR, was ordered on to Lauenberg. Here the leading tank commander reported that the railway bridge over the river was intact but there was a force of about 200 Germans and one Tiger tank on this side of the river. C Squadron and a company of the KSLI closed in on the bridge, hoping to prevent sabotage but, only a few hundred yards from it, the bridge was blown, sinking noisily into the river. After a short action with the enemy rearguard, around 100 prisoners were taken, including the crew of the Tiger tank who had not been able to take part in any of the action, being completely out of petrol and ammunition.

The next few days were spent in sporadic actions clearing up small villages with infantry companies supported by a few tanks. The villages were found to be only defended by small garrisons of infantry with one or two anti-tank guns. Their morale was low, resistance only half-hearted and they presented no great problem.

During one such action a prisoner-of-war camp was overrun and to my great surprise contained several 3RTR men who had been captured at Calais in 1940. Among them was a particular sergeant pal, Socker Heath. He clambered up onto my tank, grabbed me by the hand and said, 'I always knew the 3rd would come for me.'

By the end of April two bridges across the River Elbe had been completed and the division was ordered to cross on 30 April. Excellent progress was made and on 5 May 3RTR and 4KSLI entered Bad Segeberg. The 23rd Hussars and the 8th Rifle Brigade were pressing on for Travemünde and Neustadt and the 2nd Fife and Forfar Yeomanry with 1st Cheshires were directed onto Lubeck.

We were all rather surprised when the order to halt came: the suspension of all action coming over our radios. We were then told by official announcement that Field Marshal Montgomery had accepted the surrender of all enemy forces facing the Second Army Group. The news of the total surrender to the Allies followed two days later.

To all intents and purposes the war was over and it seemed to most of the tank crews to be rather an anti-climax. There was some clearing up to be done, odd isolated German units were being rounded up by the German 8th Parachute Division, which had already surrendered, but 3RTR was told that a strong force of SS troops were holed up in Segeberg Forst, refusing to surrender other than to a British unit. A squadron of tanks was required to assist in rounding up the German unit. I drew the short straw and duly set out with my squadron and a company of the KSLI for Segeberg Forst – not without some trepidation, as we had enjoyed a considerable celebration party the night before and I was not feeling my best.

However, there were no difficulties. We found the SS unit to be a complete anti-tank battalion recently returned from the Russian front. They were drawn up in full array, officers in dress uniform, almost as if for inspection. Getting out of my tank I approached the senior officers standing in front of their troops.

Immediately one of them stepped forward and in perfect English said: 'My colonel will only surrender his unit to a British officer of field rank!'

However, I was able to assure him that I was of field rank and this was borne out by seventeen tanks of my squadron now surrounding his unit. I told him I would be pleased to accept his colonel's sword and revolver. In convoy, we escorted the complete unit back to Bad Segeberg, the colonel and his adjutant riding on the front of my tank.

On inspection it was found that the anti-tank guns were equipped with a special sighting gear which enabled them to fire with complete accuracy at night. One of the guns with its equipment was immediately shipped back to the UK for further examination.

We spent several more weeks in Bad Segeberg before being detailed for containment duties along the Eiderstadt, where all the northern German forces were encamped prior to their demobilisation.

It was a strange time for 3RTR. Changes in the battalion happened almost daily, war-time officers and men were being demobilised and squadrons were soon down to skeleton strength. Many senior officers who had been away in Staff positions and on military missions, etc. felt it expedient to return to regimental duty in order to retain their seniority and possibly gain command. Consequently, I very soon found myself relegated to second-in-command of a squadron, with very little possibility of a regular commission.

When I was commissioned in the field in 1942 I was granted an emergency commission with the promise of a regular commission at the end of hostilities. This was now not forthcoming – although I attended a War Office selection board in Hanover, gaining a reasonable result, the commission I so wanted did not materialise. As an alternative I was offered another five years' short-service commission or a return to the ranks in the rank of WO I (regimental sergeant major). I declined the offer and decided to leave 3RTR, joining the military government.

It was a sad moment, for I had been with 3RTR from 1933 onwards, throughout its operations in Calais in 1940, the Western Desert, Greece and from Normandy to the Baltic.

Epilogue

3RTR had now moved into barracks in Flensberg, engaged in more or less peacetime duties. In October 1945 I joined a military government detachment in Kiel, where, still in my temporary rank of major, I was appointed president of summary courts, sitting in Kiel and Flensberg.

After almost a year I was posted to 930K detachment, stationed at Husum on the west coast of Schleswig-Holstein. I was second-in-command of the detachment and my duties included helping to reorganise the German transport system, both road and rail. It was a very interesting time but I was becoming more and more disillusioned with military government.

Whilst on a few days' leave in Hamburg, I met an old army friend, Lieutenant Colonel Freddie Spencer-Chapman. He was now headmaster of the British school in Plon and he said, 'I'm looking for a bursar. Do you want the job?' I leapt at the chance and within a couple of weeks I had managed to obtain the transfer. At the same time I also applied for my discharge from the regular army but applied for a commission in the Territorial Army. This eventually came through and I was commissioned as a captain in the TA.

I had a few days' leave in England whilst these events were being finalised, before returning to Germany as a civilian to take up my duties as bursar at the King Alfred School in Plon.

After some two and a half very pleasant years in Plon my duties at the school were terminated and I returned to the UK. I applied for several bursarships without success, so, once again, I applied for a regular commission – this time with the Royal Electrical and Mechanical Engineers. I was eventually accepted in the rank of second lieutenant and joined the Depot REME at Arborfiela on 28 May 1951. In all I completed twelve years with REME, retiring in April 1962 in the rank of major, and on a pension instead of a gratuity.

My association with the Royal Tank Regiment is still maintained through the various branches of the Old Comrades Association. 3RTR, sadly, is no more, having been amalgamated with 2RTR, and the regiment is now down to two battalions only. Having visited 2RTR stationed in Fallingbostel, Germany recently, I find the spirit of 3RTR lives on: the tank crews are in good heart and I am quite sure that, should the need arise, they will uphold the traditions of the war-time Royal Tank Regiment.

A Wearing Of The Green

Oh, Paddy Hehir did you hear the griff that's in the air,
That the Yo Yo boys have won the war and the 3rd Tanks were
    not there,
Oh, the Staffs were first in Mersa and the Notts they took Matruh,
When both led to Bhengazi oh, then where the hell were you?
Miles and miles ahead of them a 'probin' Jerry's screen,
A Tank Corps crew far up the 'blue', a wearing of the green.

You remember in September when we battered Jerry's flanks,
The Notts ran out of petrol and the Staffs ran out of tanks,
For the Grants they shot the Cruisers up and Jerry shot the Grants,
But the best of what was left did with 'Crisp' column get its chance,
As they swarmed around Himamel learned to see and not be seen,
With the Tank Corps crew far up the 'blue', a wearing of the green.

When Rommel came to Alamein and Monty rolled him back,
Two famous Gee-Gee regiments were first in the attack,
Oh, the press was full of praises and the flicks were full of shots,
Of the story of the Staffords and the glory of the Notts,
But miles and miles ahead of them a 'probin' Jerry's screen,
A Tank Corps crew far up the 'blue', a wearing of the green.

Now when we came to Tripoli and toured around the town,
They went and told the story of the 8th Brigade's renown,
Oh, they named the Greys, they named the Notts, the Staffords
    they did name,
And how they formed the spearhead all the way from Alamein,

163

But they never named the boys who first upon the scene,
A Tank Corps crew far up the 'blue', a wearing of the green.

Oh, the 8th Hussars they sailed back home for the Victory Parade,
And the Gloucesters and the CLY with their medals well displayed,
Oh, the 10th Hussars were shining and the Lancers spruce and spare,
And the boys were all bull-shitting, but the 3rd Tanks they were where?
Miles and miles behind them digging a latrine,
A Tank Corps crew still up the 'blue', a wearing of the green.

Oh, now we wear a Fox's mask but once instead of that,
We did display so bright and gay a crimson desert rat,
And when the show is over and friends ask about the war,
Our proudest claim we have to fame and the proudest badge we bore,
Is the little tank upon our sleeve and the flashes that are to be seen,
On any 3rd Tank crew from the desert 'blue', a wearing of the green.

This was penned after the North African Campaign. 3RTR left the 'Desert Rats' of 7th Armoured Division and joined 8th Armoured Brigade. The author is anonymous but obviously aggrieved at the lack of recognition for the 3rd's efforts. 'Paddy' Hehir, MBE was the 3RTR regimental sergeant major in 1941 and quartermaster from 1942 to 1951.